I'm Glad You Asked That

Books by Rita and Dennis Bennett

THE HOLY SPIRIT AND YOU

THE HOLY SPIRIT AND YOU: TEACHING MANUAL

I'm Glad You Asked That

Rita Bennett

Timely Questions Women Ask
About the Christian Life

Illustrated by Jean Beers

Aglow/Logos Publications
Edmonds, Wa./Plainfield, N.J.

Bible quotations are taken from the King James Version of the Bible except where otherwise indicated. Many King James quotations have been modernized for clarity.

In all Bible quotations (except TAB), italics and bracketed insertions have been supplied by the author.

Abbreviations used for other versions:

ASV	American Standard Version
au. para.	author's paraphrase
NASB	New American Standard Bible
NEB	New English Bible
NGT	The Interlinear Greek-English New Testament: The Nestle Greek Text with a Literal English Translation by . . . Alfred Marshall
RSV	Revised Standard Version
TAB	The Amplified Bible
TLB	The Living Bible

Cover photography and design by Katie Fortune.

Copyright © 1974 by Aglow/Logos Publications
Edmons, Wa./Plainfield, N.J.
All rights reserved
Printed in the United States of America
Library of Congress Catalog Card Number: 74-81754
ISBN: 088270-090-1 (cloth), 088270-084-7 (paper)

This book is dedicated with great love
to my husband, Dennis, who keeps me "glad
he asked that question."

Special Thanks:
To the *Aglow* editors, Pat King and Jo Anne
Sekowsky, love and thanks in the Lord for their
helpful advice and encouragement during the
writing of this book. Thanks also to my dear secretary, Janet Koether, who so painstakingly typed and
retyped the manuscript and shared a personal
interest in the work.

CONTENTS

Foreword

We are told that the written law alone kills, but the Spirit gives life (II Cor. 3:6). In this book, Rita Bennett has shown wisdom in a balanced presentation, using the Word and the Spirit to teach truth and help develop proper attitudes. She has taken vital, practical questions from Christian women and has done an excellent job of dealing with the heart of their problems.

I appreciate the methods she has used throughout the book to minister to spirit, soul, and body, helping women to be whole. Consistent with Paul's teaching, she shows how we enter into God's rest by applying the Scripture to our lives. Hebrews 4:12 tells us, "The Word of God is quick, and powerful, and sharper than any two-edged sword, piercing even to the dividing asunder of soul and spirit, and of the joints and marrow, and is a discerner of the thoughts and intents of the heart."

Today, we need the kind of spiritual guidance that Rita has given to help combat the forces of darkness that are leading many women to destruction. No matter where you are in your Christian walk, I believe that you will benefit greatly from reading I'm Glad You Asked That!

Shirley Boone

Preface

Christian women have the difficult task of being witnesses to their husbands and other family members, as well as to the world. In this book, I've tried to show that the way you conduct your life is your most powerful witness to unbelievers. As you "live the life" consistently, in time there will come the questions: "How can you be so peaceful all the time?" "Why don't you gossip like other women do?" "Why do I feel such a restfulness in your home?"

When such questions have opened the door, you may think to yourself, "I'm glad you asked that question." Then speaking unhurriedly with the guidance of the Holy Spirit give the answer.

Most of the questions answered in this book have come through my experience in teaching Bible classes, speaking to women's groups, and sharing with my husband in radio programs in Los Angeles and Seattle over a period of eight years. Other questions have come from letters and from personal counseling sessions. All the major Scripture issues concerning women are dealt with here, as well as the questions women most frequently ask about interpersonal relationships.

The answers are given in the light of Scripture, the only reliable guide of conduct, and in the light of history which gives further understanding of Scripture. Christian women want God's truth, not man's theory, and this book was written for women who are already believers in the divinity of Jesus Christ, although I trust that others may also find it helpful.

I am grateful for all I learned while doing library research for many of the answers, and also for the exciting, fresh, and brand-new understanding given directly by the Holy Spirit. I hope and pray that after you've read, *I'm Glad You Asked That!* you'll say, "I'm glad I read that!" God bless you.

In the Love of Jesus,
Rita Bennett

THE

SINGLE

GIRL

DUNAMIS!

Holy Spirit Power . . .

Receiving God's Power to Resist Temptation

Dear Rita,

I am a junior in college and have been secretly in love with and sneaking off to date one of my professors, who is a married man. Although we haven't gotten to the point of having an affair, we are headed in that direction. Since hearing about the reality of God experienced through the Baptism in the Holy Spirit, I'm beginning to wonder if this might be what I need to be able to be a stronger Christian, and resist things that I know are wrong. I want to pray for this experience with God but know I can't while living out of Christ's will for my life. What can I do? I really love this man, but I also love Jesus, and I know His will for my life couldn't include this relationship.

Dear Tempted Collegiate,

The very fact that you've asked this question shows that the Holy Spirit is at work in your life. I'm sure you've already realized that you would never be truly happy sneaking around as a mistress to your professor. I'm also sure you wouldn't want to cause the breakup of his present marriage.

Often young women who have not received normal love and affection in their formative years are easy prey to men who are more than willing to meet their need for love. I don't know if this is your case or not, but if so, Jesus is the only one who can truly

3

meet that deep need you have to be loved. To paraphrase St. Augustine, "God has made you for Himself and you'll be restless until you find your rest in Him." Receiving the Baptism with the Holy Spirit* is the best way I know for a Christian to deepen his experience of God. This experience heightens your awareness of and fellowship with God and therefore fulfills your life in a new way. For this reason, some have called it a baptism of love.

The Baptism in the Holy Spirit will help you. Jesus knew His people would have great temptations, and He did not leave us powerless against these things. Even after His resurrection, and after He had breathed eternal life into His first followers, He commanded them to wait until they received the Baptism with the Holy Spirit (Acts 1:4-5). They were already born again of the Spirit, but they hadn't received the *power* Jesus knew they would need. Jesus' final recorded words on earth were these: "But you shall receive power when the Holy Spirit has come upon you; and you shall be My witnesses both in Jerusalem, and in all Judea and Samaria, and even to the remotest part of the earth" (Acts 1:8 NASB).

To understand the importance of the gift of the Holy Spirit, consider these final instructions that Jesus shared with His loved ones. He knew they were going to need *power* (Greek *dunamis*, from

---

*I use the terms Baptism *with* the Holy Spirit and Baptism *in* the Holy Spirit interchangeably, since *in* and *with* are interchangeable in the Greek.

which we get the word "dynamite") in order to make it as witnesses. The fact that these were His final recorded words has great significance to me. If you were chosen to be one of the first passengers to travel to the moon, your final words to your loved ones just before you blasted off would be well-chosen, wouldn't they? They wouldn't be about trivia, but about the most helpful and most important things for your loved ones. That's the way it was with Jesus.

Luke not only tells about this at the beginning of the Book of Acts, but he says it in a slightly different way in his Gospel of Luke: "And behold, I am sending forth the promise of My Father upon you; but you are to stay in the city until you are clothed with power from on high" (Luke 24:49 NASB).

Many young people who have faced circumstances similar to yours would have been saved numerous heartaches and tragic mistakes if only someone had told them about the power of the Spirit. It is sad to see youths who are led to a saving knowledge of Jesus and are not told about praying for the power to live the life. It's much like putting a soldier on the battlefield and not giving him any weapons.

I'm glad someone told you about God's power so that the tragedy you were headed for will not occur. You've already made your choice for Jesus by your request for advice. It is not practical to go into detail in this letter, preparing you to receive the Baptism with the Holy Spirit; instead, I'm going to recommend that you read the first five chapters of *The Holy Spirit and You*, a book on this subject by my husband and myself.* If you can find someone to help you pray for this blessing, fine, but you can pray all by yourself, since Jesus is the Baptizer and has already become your Savior.

After receiving the power of the Holy Spirit, your most active defense against the enemy and his temptations will be to stay in close fellowship with God, and empowered Christians. Attend a Spirit-filled prayer meeting at least once a week. The Scriptures give us guidance for our lives, so be sure you are reading the Bible. It would be good to purchase a modern translation, such as the New American Standard Bible, The Living Bible, or The Amplified Bible and read from it regularly. Get into a good Bible study group if at all possible, and attend church each week.

It is important that you do not talk to your professor in any secluded place. You might give him a copy of a book of testimony about meeting Jesus as Savior and Baptizer, and just tell him that what the book tells about has happened to you, and you won't be seeing him anymore. It may mean his salvation and that of his marriage. Avoid going to places that would tempt you to reminisce about some of the good times you had together. Don't listen to music that makes you think of him and pulls at your heartstrings. Meditate on this Scrip-

*Dennis and Rita Bennett, *The Holy Spirit and You* (Plainfield, N.J.: Logos International, 1971).

ture: "No temptation has overtaken you but such as is common to man: and God is faithful, who will not allow you to be tempted beyond what you are able; but with the temptation will provide the way of escape also, that you may be able to endure it" (I Cor. 10:13 NASB).

The Lord has provided your way of escape, so take it. As you do, He will provide the right man for you—one who doesn't belong to someone else. Keep yourself for him. You'll be glad you did.

Now get ready to blast off into a new dimension in the Christian life. You'll find that the pull of earth will be less and less powerful as you "go into orbit" with the Lord.

P.S. to readers: After this young lady reaffirmed her faith in Jesus, and asked the Lord's forgiveness, she was beautifully baptized with the Holy Spirit and great joy.

Sex Education

Dear Rita,

I am a Christian, twenty-one years old and engaged to be married. I have had very little sex education and don't feel prepared for the physical part of marriage. Neither my mother, minister, nor medical doctor have given me any practical advice. All my doctor did, in addition to giving me a physical examination, was to suggest birth-control pills if I wasn't interested in having children right away. I know books on sex are all over the newsstands, but I'd be embarrassed to buy one of them, and if I did, I would not be sure whether or not it had a Christian viewpoint. Can you help me?

Dear Engaged,

Christians in the past have fallen down in their responsibility to provide sex education for young people. Most Christian books written in this field have been idealistic but not practical and truly helpful. I'm glad to say, however, there are now an increasing number of concerned and brave people tackling this subject and coming up with some excellent books.

The first book I would recommend is *Sexual Happiness in Marriage*, by Dr. Herbert J. Miles, published by Zondervan. Dr. Miles has been a leading marriage counselor for twenty years. He suggests his book be read by couples within three weeks to three months of their wedding date. The book is also recommended for the already married who are having difficulty helping one another to find fulfillment. The author wrote for the person who hadn't had thorough premarital counseling, which fits your situation exactly. This is a very sound book which I'm sure will answer many questions for you. It doesn't go into great detail on the courtship period, but gives practical advice beginning with the honeymoon and continuing on through parenthood.

I have also been impressed with the book, *I Married You*, by Walter Trobisch, published by Harper and Row. Mr. Trobisch is a European pastor and marriage counselor who talks about the problems of courtship and marriage in a refreshing and candid way. His book is based on real life problems which confronted him when he was asked to speak on Christian marriage to a church congregation in Africa. Another book by the same author is called *Please Help Me! Please Love Me!* It presents a Christian view of contraception.

A book which ranges from courtship and marital happiness, to adjusting to children, has the ironic title, *How To Be Happy Though Married*. It was written by Tim LaHaye and is published by Tyndale House. Much of what this book contains is already covered in the first book I mentioned; however, it has quite a bit more to say on the courtship period.

I believe these four books will give you good basic knowledge. If you apply their truths, you and your husband should have a good beginning for a successful marriage all the way through.

Mr. Right will be along and at the right time too!

Meeting Eligible Males

Dear Rita,

I am a college graduate in my early twenties. Several years ago I received Jesus as my Savior and a short time later as Baptizer in the Holy Spirit.

As a school teacher, I find it difficult to meet eligible young men to date. Those who have asked me out are not Christians, much less living in the power of the Holy Spirit. Like any woman my age, I long to be happily married, to have a family, and a place of my own. Presently I am dating a young businessman who is an agnostic but claims he doesn't mind if I practice Christianity. Our friendship has been growing over several months of dating.

I'm aware that the Scripture warns against being unequally yoked together with unbelievers, but what if "Mr. Right" never comes along, and I'm left in the lurch?

Dear Teach,

The most important thing for you to decide at this time is whether you want God's first best plan for your life, or something less than that. A woman can go on with God and be married to an unbeliever, but it's not easy. Also, there's a part of yourself which can never be shared with an unbeliever, and therefore there cannot be complete oneness in the spirit as well as in the soul and body. All three are important.

Recently I was talking to an older woman who shared this sad story of her early life: "I was raised in an isolated small town. Eligible young men were scarce. I began dating a young man who could talk the Christian 'lingo,' but seemingly had no experience of God. Because of the hypocrisy in the lives of some people close to me, and because I was dating this young man, I began to cool down in my own dedication to Christ. One night I had a dream or vision of a handsome young man and was shown by the Lord that this was the one I was meant to marry. As time passed, I increasingly doubted the possibility of this occurring and, in haste, married the man I was dating. Three weeks later, the one God had chosen for me arrived in our little town. He was a traveling evangelist, the grandson of a great Christian leader. This young man told someone that if he had arrived three weeks before, my last name would have been his."

This woman had no idea that her husband would turn out to be an alcoholic, leaving home on weekends regularly and making her life and the lives of their children miserable much of the time. Instead of her musical talent being used for God all those years (the evangelist was also talented musically), she has had to wait until the senior years of life to share her talents worldwide. What misery could have been averted; what joy could have been received!

As the saying goes, "There's something worse than not being married, and that's being married to the wrong man." Nevertheless, God has placed this desire for marriage in your heart, and I believe He will give you your heart's desire.

Perhaps it would be a good idea to look at the Scripture to which you referred in your letter *in toto:* "Be not unequally yoked together with unbelievers: for what fellowship has righteousness with unrighteousness? And what communion has light with darkness? And what concord has Christ with Belial? Or what part has he that believes with an infidel? And what agreement has the temple of God with idols? For you are the temple of the living God; as God has said, I will dwell in them, and walk in them; and I will be their God, and they shall be my people" (II Cor. 6:14-16). Although these verses are not speaking only of marriage, yet they are certainly applicable to it as well as to other personal relationships.

Another significant Scripture verse is, "Jesus . . . said . . . Every kingdom divided against itself is brought to desolation; and every city or house divided against itself shall not stand" (Matt. 12:25).

There are enough things to adjust to in marriage without inviting the obvious problems of being unequally yoked. Even in Christian marriage, there are plenty of adjustments to make. My further advice to you and other young women who are baptized with the Holy Spirit is to marry a man with the same experience, someone who is actually *walking* in this empowering experience. For me, there would be something lacking in our marriage if my husband

and I could not pray and sing in the Spirit together as well as share in daily Bible reading and intercessory prayer. Your husband should be the spiritual head of your home and take the responsibility for daily family devotions. It is a good idea to begin the practice of shared prayer and Bible reading during your courtship.

A young woman from our church was seriously dating a young man, and it looked like an engagement was soon to be announced. Fortunately, our youth group was studying Scripture and discussing what Christian marriage should be like. When she saw the verse about wives being expected to submit to their husbands "as unto the Lord" (Eph. 5:22), the young lady realized she would have to have confidence in her husband's relationship to the Lord. Because she did not have that confidence about the young man she was dating, their relationship was terminated. The right man came along later that year. Now she is happily married.

Have you shared your testimony with your present suitor? Have you shared some good charismatic books with him, for example, Pat Boone's *A New Song*, or George Otis' *High Adventure*, or my husband's *Nine O'Clock in the Morning*? Have you invited him to your church and/or prayer group? All these things are good tests to see if he has any openness to the Lord and to present him with the opportunity to receive the same new life and power you have received. Of course, you could marry him as is and hope for the best, but you would be taking a *big risk.* If he shows no interest in a Jesus-centered life, drop him, but fast!

To meet those with like faith, get involved with a charismatic home prayer group under responsible leadership, or help to get one started for people your age. Many churches are now sponsoring interdenominational young unmarried groups, often meeting in restaurants or other secular locations. The denomination your husband-to-be comes from is not so important, but he should be a true born-again believer, baptized in the Holy Spirit.

Another Scripture which comes to mind for you is, "Seek ye first the kingdom of God . . . and all these things shall be added unto you" (Matt. 6:33). If you put God first in your life, all these other blessings will be added. If you put marriage first, you may very possibly miss God's best plan for your life. It is God's desire to give you complete fulfillment in every area—spiritually, mentally, and physically.

Don't let the enemy scare you with the idea that you must accept the first interested suitor. It isn't wise to rush into a lifelong relationship. Remember, the enemy drives the sheep, but the Lord Jesus leads them.

As you put the Lord first in your life, you can at the same time make yourself available in places where eligible males are, keep your weight normal, and dress attractively. I believe I'm not wrong when I say, "Mr. Right will be along, and at the right time too!"

Virginity

Dear Rita,

What's the good of being a virgin before marriage? It seems that only puritanical people think such a standard is important anymore. Recently a minister told a friend of mine that marriage will be outmoded in the next ten years, so it won't matter anyway. So many books, movies, and magazines encourage free love today, that I'm beginning to think I've been rather square. Do you think Christians should change with the times?

Dear Rather Square,

When Paul teaches about the marriage relationship, he compares it to the relationship between Jesus and His people. Often in the Scripture, God uses the picture of marital fidelity as a type of His faithfulness, and/or His people's faithfulness or unfaithfulness to Him. In the Old Testament, we find some toleration of polygamy—a man having more than one wife—but this is far from God's original plan, one woman for one man. However, we find no toleration of premarital sex. Indeed, it is so far from the thinking of the Scripture that people should cohabit without marriage, that we cannot find in the Bible any examples of the kind of thing that is happening so much today; that is, where a couple who are not even necessarily intending to marry, have sexual intercourse simply as a part of the dating process.

The nearest thing we can find in the Bible to this is the tragic case of Dinah, Jacob's daughter. The pagan prince Shechem took Dinah, "lay with her and defiled her" (Gen. 34:2). True, Shechem wanted to marry her, but to be unequally yoked with an idolater and unbeliever was forbidden to God's people. The sons of Jacob were so furious when they learned what had happened to Dinah that they killed Shechem and all the men of the city and brought their sister home. These drastic measures reflect the uncompromising attitude of the Old Testament toward sex outside of marriage. And this wasn't because of a prudish or puritanical attitude toward sex. Sex was considered good, to be enjoyed, but it was also very sacred, and carefully regulated and controlled because it was so important to the propagation of the race and the strength of the family.

Most other cases of sex outside marriage in the Bible involve either prostitution or rape.

Amnon, one of King David's sons, thought he was "in love" with his half-brother Absalom's sister, Tamar (II Sam. 13). This beautiful virgin was tricked into taking care of Amnon when he feigned illness. He forced her to have sexual relations with him and then immediately turned against her, hating her more than he once thought he loved her. Amnon's so-called love was only selfish sexual desire. He was willing to ruin a life for a moment of temporary satisfaction. The further tragedy was that Absalom, resenting David's failure to administer discipline, took revenge by having Amnon killed, and then went on to rebel against his father.

There is nothing in the Bible to condone a double standard of sexual behavior. It's just as important for men to keep themselves for their wives as it is for women to keep themselves for their husbands. The outcome of an episode in Joseph's life shows the honor that comes to those who are faithful to God's standards.

Potiphar's wife tried to seduce Joseph, a virtuous man, who had been set by her husband as head servant of his household. When Joseph rebuffed her advances, she ripped off his coat as he ran from her. She then showed the coat to Potiphar, an influential officer in Pharaoh's army, claiming it as evidence that Joseph had sexually attacked her. Because of her lie, Joseph was imprisoned, but by God's intervention, he was set free and raised to great power and influence in Egypt—next in authority to Pharaoh over all the land.

Premarital sex in the modern sense is neither rape—both parties are consenting—nor prostitution—there is no commercialism involved. The word in the Scripture for it is "fornication," a word taken from the Greek *porneia* (from which we get "pornography"), which means any kind of sexual misbehavior. Paul speaks to the Corinthians: "I wrote you in a letter not to be close friends with fornicators— yet not to entirely avoid the fornicators of the world

. . . because you would have to leave the world entirely!—but I told you in a litter not to associate with a *brother* who is known to be a fornicator, or a greedy man, or an idol-worshipper, or abusive person, or a drunkard, or an unscrupulous person—with such people, no, don't even sit down to eat! . . . Remove the evil out of your midst" (I Cor. 5:9-11, 13b free translation from Greek).

Again he admonishes them, "Don't you know that people who live wrongly won't inherit the Kingdom of God? Don't be fooled: neither fornicators, nor idol-worshippers, nor adulterers, nor catamites [male homosexuals who allow themselves to be used by other males] nor sodomites [male homosexuals who abuse other males], nor thieves, nor greedy people, nor swindlers, will inherit the Kingdom of God; and some of you were these things, but you were washed, you were made holy, you were justified in the Name of the Lord Jesus Christ and by the Spirit of our God. . . . Run away from fornication; other sins which a person commits are separate from his body (outside his body), but he who commits fornication sins against his own body. Don't you know that your body is a temple (sanctuary, shrine) for the Holy Spirit Who is in you, Whom you have from God? And you don't belong to yourselves, because you have been bought with a price? So give God glory in your body (I Cor. 6:9-11, 18-20 free translation from Greek).

Paul counsels believers not to have close fellowship with fornicators of the world, but to have *no* fellowship with fornicators who are believers and who continue unrepentantly in this pattern of behavior. Hopefully, this kind of ostracism will help to bring them to their senses and to repentance, so that they can be restored to the fellowship.

Some may think the Bible is just being narrow. No, there are plenty of reasons for prohibitions against premarital sex. Sex is not an end in itself, but is an expression of true love and fidelity. It can rightly be engaged in only within the bonds of the marriage vows. In "free love," the woman is always the loser. The modern "freedom" of sex really means the freedom of the man to get what he wants without any responsibilities to go with it. The girl wants love, companionship, warmth, and out of this will grow the ability to respond and have sexual satisfaction within the safety of marriage.

Girls who are persuaded to "have sex" on a date are usually cheated in more ways than one, for not only is their psyche harmed, and perhaps they may become pregnant, but also they will rarely enjoy the experience, because it is fraught with anxiety which militates against the female response. The man has his physical kicks, because the male does not have the same kind of needs or inhibitions about sex. However, he is still harming himself whether he knows it or not. Don't let anyone talk you into it. If a man doesn't want you for yourself, don't be persuaded to give him your body for his use. I agree with Shirley Boone who says in her book, *One Woman's Liberation*, "The only *free love* around that I know about is described in John 3:16: 'For God so loved the world that He gave his only begotten Son, that whosoever believes in Him should not perish, but have everlasting life!' "*

The question may be asked, "What about the man you think you will marry?" If he loves you, will he demand that you cohabit with him before marriage? The fact that he suggests it does not prove he does not love you—it may merely prove he is stupid or thoughtless, or just going along with the thinking of the crowd, or has the currently popular but mistaken idea that he must have sex. If you refuse him and he leaves, you know that he did not really love you anyway. You have lost nothing.

What of the people who have already gone this route, who have already been taken in by the new morality (which is really the "old immorality") and have been promiscuous with a number of partners. Are they ruined?

The wonderful thing about Jesus is that when we turn to Him and ask to be forgiven, He cleanses us from all sins—big and little—and makes us into new creatures. He not only forgives our sins but forgets them.

The story of Rahab, the harlot (Josh. 2; 6:25), shows us an outstanding picture of the grace of God. When the children of Israel were coming to Jericho to possess the land promised to them, they sent two spies to investigate and see how difficult

*Shirley Boone, One Woman's Liberation (Carol Stream, Illinois: Creation House, 1972).

the job would be. The two spies lodged at Rahab's house, which was situated on the wall of the city.* The king suspected where they were and sent some soldiers to capture them, but Rahab, who had come to believe in their God, hid the spies. As a result, they promised to save her and all her family if she would tie a scarlet rope in her front window—the same rope with which she helped them escape over the wall. (This scarlet rope can be seen as a symbol of the blood of Jesus whereby *all* who believe in and receive Jesus may be saved.) But Rahab was not only saved physically in the destruction of Jericho, her previous life was forgiven her. Later, she married an Israelite named Salmon, became the mother of Boaz, who in turn was the husband of Ruth, and the grandfather of King David. Rahab, the harlot, forgiven, became an ancestress in the direct line of the Lord Jesus Christ Himself (Matt. 1:5). She is recorded in what some have called "God's Old Testament Hall of Fame," the eleventh chapter of Hebrews, as one of the commendable women (Heb. 11:31). The story of Rahab and what God can do in a repentant life should encourage any who have had a checkered past.

I believe we should observe scriptural guidelines rather than the thinking of a fallen world. Many young people are floundering for lack of standards. You are told to "do your own thing," but

---

*This did not imply that the men were seeking her service as a prostitute. Probably she ran a type of hotel, and it was the closest lodging inside the gate of the wall.

you will have much happier memories, fewer psychological scars to be healed, and will derive deeper enjoyment from your marriage if you will keep yourself for your own husband.

No, Christians should not change with the times, but rather should change the times to fit into God's plans and purposes.

THE

MARRIED

WOMAN

O.K. to talk now, Lord?

Communicating with Your Husband

Dear Rita,

I have been married for a little over a year, and know I have much to learn about getting along with my husband. Mealtime is supposed to be a relaxed, happy time, but often at our house it's just the opposite. If I bring up any problem at all, it's usually the straw that breaks the camel's back—just one too many. How am I going to share necessary concerns with my husband when he gets so upset every time I do so?

Dear Needing-to-Communicate,

To answer your question, the best scriptural analogy I can think of is the story of how Jesus handled the situation with Peter, when He needed to have a little talk with him. Peter, who always had great intentions, had said he was willing even to die with Jesus. Yet at the last minute, three times he denied even *knowing* Him.

We read in John of Jesus' third appearance to His disciples after His resurrection. Peter was back at his old trade of being a fisherman. He must have reasoned, "After all, Jesus didn't bring in the kingdom as we thought He would, and I have to make a living some way." That night the fishing was totally unproductive, and Jesus, standing on the shore, shouted for them to cast the net on the opposite side of the boat. When they did so, the nets were immediately filled with so many fish that the disciples thought the nets would break. When John told the others that the man on the shore was Jesus, Peter threw himself into the water and swam to Him.

Jesus didn't immediately say to Peter, "You're just the one I've wanted to see. I'm displeased with you and the way you denied knowing Me. Sit down and let's have a talk." Instead, Jesus said to Peter, and the other disciples as they arrived on shore, "Let's have something to eat." This was wisdom. He knew they had fished all night and were tired. Jesus must have done a little fishing Himself, for when the disciples arrived, they found enough fish for all of them grilling on the fire. After Peter was well fed, dried off, and warmed by the fire, then Jesus began to talk to him.

This is a good pattern for you and for all wives. When your husband comes home from a hectic day at his work, he needs time to make a transition from his job to his home. Greet him at the door with your love and encouragement. Dinner should be nearly ready. During the meal, keep the conversation pleasant. After he's been well fed and has had some time to relax and read the paper, share your concerns with him. Always preface the problem, especially if he's in some way involved, with some appreciative, relationship-strengthening conversation: "Thanks for taking time to pick up those groceries for me." "You are a wonderful husband. It was so thoughtful of you to phone and let me know you'd be a little late for supper." Perhaps you will sit on the arm of his chair and assure him of your love. In this way, he will not feel so threatened when you bring up the problem.

Jesus not only fed the disciples physically, but He fed them spiritually as well. You can feed your husband in the same way. During the day, while your husband is at work, you can be receiving spiritual nourishment from the Lord. Spend all the time you can feeding on His words. Listen to Scripture on tape or taped faith-building teaching and testimonies while you iron, sew, or run taxi service to and from school, or when driving to the grocery store. When your husband comes home from work, he will feel refreshed by the presence of Christ in you. You will find yourself sharing words of life rather than bits of negative gossip.

Who knows? You yourself may be so refreshed by the heightened awareness of Jesus within you, that even the "problem" you needed to air will have turned into an avenue of blessing for both of you. As Jesus said, "With men this is impossible; but with God all things are possible" (Matt. 19:26).

All things are possible, even happy meals with joyful fellowship around the supper table.

Sexual Fulfillment

Dear Rita,

I have been married four years and have a very kind and loving husband. Recently, through reading on the subject of sexual adjustment in marriage, I came to understand that women were supposed to enjoy complete sexual fulfillment. Giving myself physically to my husband is nice, and I feel my wifely duty, but I never expected more than a sense of belonging, and the satisfaction of meeting my husband's needs. Does this idea of the sexual climax for the wife have a Christian basis or only a secular one?

Dear Dutiful Wife,

In the past, many groups in the Christian faith have denied that God approves of sexual pleasure for both husband and wife. However, there is a new conviction in Christianity that marriage was intended to meet the sexual needs of both partners to the fullest, that not only was the woman created to meet the needs of her husband but that he would meet her needs also.

One particular confirmation in Scripture stands out in my mind, that of Sarah, Abraham's wife. When she was nearly ninety, long past the menopause, and her husband was nearly one hundred, the angel of the Lord came to tell Abraham that

Sarah, who had been barren until that time, would have a son. Sarah, who was in her tent house, overheard this conversation, and the Scripture says, "Therefore Sarah laughed within herself, saying, 'After I am waxed old shall I have pleasure, my lord being old also?' " (Gen. 18:12).

Apparently Sarah had found the marriage union a pleasurable experience.

In the New Testament, Sarah is set up as an example for Christian wives to follow: "For after this manner in the old time the holy women also, who trusted in God, adorned themselves [inwardly], being in subjection [voluntary subjection in love] unto their own husbands; Even as Sarah obeyed Abraham, calling him lord [sir]: whose daughters you are, as long as you do well . . . (I Pet. 3:5-6).

The clearest passage in the New Testament teaching basic truths on sexual adjustment for the Christian is found in Paul's letter to the Corinthians: "The husband should give to his wife her conjugal [sexual] rights, and likewise the wife to her husband. For the wife does not rule over her own body, but the husband does; likewise the husband does not rule over his own body, but the wife does. Do not refuse one another except perhaps by agreement for a season, that you may devote yourselves to prayer; but then come together again, lest Satan tempt you through lack of self-control"(I Cor. 7:3-5 RSV).

This passage indicates that both husband and wife have definite sexual needs to be met in mar-

31

riage. The Victorian idea that sex was to be enjoyed only by the man, the wife simply putting up with it, is erroneous in the light of the Bible and of scientific fact. Note that this scripture doesn't say the wife is to meet her own sexual needs, nor does it say the husband is supposed to meet his own sexual needs, but it does say that they are to meet one another's mutual needs.

Another interesting point is that the couple's conjugal life is shown as being related to their prayer life. Apparently, a mutually satisfying married life in the physical realm does not conflict with a devout spiritual life.

The Book of Proverbs puts it beautifully: "Drink waters out of thine own cistern, and running waters out of thine own well. Let thy fountain be blessed: and rejoice with the wife of thy youth. Let her be as the loving hind and pleasant roe; let her breasts satisfy thee at all times; and be thou ravished always with her love" (Prov. 5:15, 18-19).

This passage indicates that in sexual union the husband is to rejoice *with* his wife, which indicates that not just one partner is enjoying it to the fullest. Procreation is not mentioned here. From this and many other verses, the Bible would seem to be saying children are a blessing to marriage but an added one to something already complete in itself.

In Genesis, that book of beginnings, after the woman was created and presented to the man, God instructed them, "Therefore shall a man *leave* his father and his mother [in the public legal action of marriage called the wedding], and shall *cleave* unto his wife [an inseparable love, "keeping only unto her]: and they shall *be one flesh* [physical union having grown out of a love relationship; the deepest act of love in a protected home situation]" (Gen. 2:24).

Jesus quotes this passage from Genesis, showing He based His thinking about marriage on it, and adds further what is recorded in the Gospels of Matthew and Mark: "They are no longer two, but one" (Matt. 19:6a; Mark 10:8b, both RSV).

This one-flesh union obviously refers to the physical union of the husband and wife in the act of love. To be one flesh indicates the same experience for both; they should have the same joy in sexual union. To be no longer two but physically one is to know what the other needs and how to satisfy him or her. Again, this passage doesn't refer to reproduction but to sex as a profound personal experience which can be experienced at its fullest only in the sheltered bonds of matrimony.

The necessary ingredients for marriage mentioned by God the Father in the Old Testament, and God the Son in the New Testament are leaving, cleaving, and being one flesh. If any one of these aspects of marriage is lacking, then the marriage is not as complete as God intended it to be.

The art of learning and entering into a mutually satisfying sexual experience requires knowledge, time, patience, and much love. It's a complex process which doesn't always happen by instinct alone.

I would encourage you and your husband to work toward the goal of mutual physical satisfaction, because when you really desire and need your husband in this way, he is bound to enjoy the marriage union more also. You and your husband would do well to do some reading together on this subject.*

In his book, *Sexual Happiness in Marriage*, Dr. Herbert Miles states that ten to twelve percent of married women in our society do not achieve a climax in sexual intercourse, but he believes a climax is the norm and God's plan for all married women. People can have very happy marriages without the sexual fulfillment of the wife, but if both partners are not working toward this goal, there would seem to be a very serious lack somewhere.

Of course, a marriage can be fulfilled in the area of the sexual life and lack fulfillment in the areas of the soul (mind, emotions, and will) and spirit (that part created for fellowship with God). The spiritual joining of a man and wife occurs when they both accept Jesus as their Savior. They are then "joined to the Lord" and become one, not only with Jesus, but with one another in spirit. The Baptism in the Holy Spirit joins husband and wife in an even fuller way in their minds and emotions. Physical union for a Christian couple should therefore be more beautiful and fulfilling than that of a marriage outside of Christ. After all, marriage was God's idea (Gen. 2:18; 1:27-28) and He saw that, "it was very good" (Gen. 1:31). Only He can make it really good in its every aspect.

*Some helpful Christian books are suggested on pp. 8-9.

Honey, you'll just love this prayer meeting!

Witnessing to Your Husband

Dear Rita,

I received the Baptism in the Holy Spirit six months ago, and I tried everything I could think of to interest my husband in it. He went to one prayer meeting, but it made him so nervous that he had to have a drink afterward. Now he doesn't even want me to mention the subject. My husband is a professed Christian, and I know how much this empowering of the Holy Spirit would mean to him if he would only open up to it. I'm anxious to know what I can do.

Dear Anxious,

You may have done too much already, but the Lord will help to redeem the situation. No blame can be attached to you for trying everything you could think of to interest your husband in this blessing of the Holy Spirit; however, there is the way of the Spirit which will gently guide your husband, or the way of man which will push him too fast and end up causing him to resist completely.

When I read your question, this story came to mind: A man sitting in his garden observed a butterfly in the process of emerging from its cocoon. After two hours of struggle, the butterfly was only halfway out. The man noted a narrow place that was restricting the butterfly. Fascinated by the

36

ongoing struggle, he took his penknife and cut open the narrow place to help the butterfly. To his sad surprise, the last third of the butterfly's body was still like a worm, with just stubs for the hind legs!

We cannot push another's spiritual growth. Each must come at his own speed. If forced, the results may be very harmful. Fortunately, the realm of the Spirit is different from the natural realm. Although the butterfly's damage could not be reversed, your husband's problem, being in the spiritual realm, can be corrected. Even our mistakes may be turned to greater good if we will release them to God—indeed, greater good than if they hadn't occurred.

The best thing to do now is to learn to rest in the Lord Jesus and step by step follow the leading of the Holy Spirit. Instead of thinking up things to do or say to interest your husband in spiritual things, establish an inward pattern of praising the Lord for what He is already doing in your husband's heart. Praise opens up the way for God to work and keeps you from being uptight, enabling God's contagious love and joy to show through you more easily.

Don't discuss your husband's inner conflicts with the entire prayer group, as this may leak back to your husband and he will never want to visit the group again. If you have one close friend who has proven discreet, you may want to confidentially share and pray about these matters with her.

Rest on this Scripture: "And we know that all things work together for good to them that love

God, to them who are the called according to His purpose" (Rom. 8:28).

Enjoying Your Home

Dear Rita,

I have four children and am a high school teacher. I went back to my job this year after staying at home for a year, and my husband threatens me with, "If our children grow up to be delinquents, it will be your fault!" He doesn't want me to continue to work, and we often have heated arguments about it. It's true we don't absolutely have to have the money—but we *both* enjoy spending it.

I worked hard to put my husband through graduate school and have helped supplement his salary for years. It seems only fair that I should have a right to determine whether I should work or not. It troubles me greatly that I spent many years acquiring advanced training (I have a Master's Degree in Counseling, and also in Education), and now my husband just wants me to stay at home and hibernate, not using the skills that God allowed me to acquire.

Dear Working Mother,

I think you should ask yourself, "Do I want to keep my husband happy (and perhaps even keep him at all), or do I want my profession instead?" The primary role of the married woman is to be a good wife, and secondly, a good mother. Everything else must work in harmony with these responsibilities and callings. I can understand how you feel in your situation, after working to help support the family for a number of years, and then all of a sudden being asked to stop.

But being a wife and mother of four children is a full-time job, and if you're working at a job away from home, *someone* is going to be neglected, no matter how hard you try. If your husband is not getting the love and companionship he needs, it may cause him to seek someone else who is more than willing to meet these needs. What your husband has expressed as his concern about the children just might take place if you are not at home more to guide them. Don't risk your marriage and the happiness of your children for your profession!

Homemaking is more than seeing that meals are cooked and the house maintained in some kind of order. It is more than just being there when the kids get home from school, or when your husband gets home from work. The mother is the queen of the household, and there is deep reassurance to the children, and to the husband, too, in knowing that she is at home while they are out on the job, or at school. The home should be, as the Book of Common Prayer calls it, "a haven of blessing and of peace," and it means a great deal to a child when he's feeling insecure, to know that he *could* go home, or call home, and mother would be there. The man has the same feelings, for all wives are also a little bit of a mother to their husbands, just as the husband is rightly something of a father to his wife. She provides the "kiss it and make it well" of a mother, while he provides the strength and protection that is a father's part. This doesn't mean that you have to stay in the house all day and wait for phone calls, but it does mean that your activities should center around the home.

Now, about your training that you feel will be wasted if you do as your husband wants you to. Be very sure that God does not waste something like that. If you will concur with your husband's wishes, in good will, you will find that God will find an application for your advanced training. Perhaps your educational background will be put to work in helping your church with its educational program, or somewhere else in the community educational picture. You might wind up on the school board. Perhaps you will find your counseling skills being exercised in helping troubled people, either through the church or through some other program in the neighborhood. Perhaps the Lord may lead you to pioneer something in these areas. There are plenty of ways to use your skills without being in full-time professional practice, and you may find yourself doing things that turn out to be even more significant and interesting, too.

I, too, was a teacher, and later a social worker. My husband, however, like yours, wants his wife at home. I have never been idle, believe me. For example, shortly after our marriage, my husband asked me to teach an adult Bible class, bringing my teaching skills into the picture. Then I began to write, using the previous experience I had had in journalism. God will not waste your talents—He may even develop new ones!

Homemaking can be challenging, fulfilling, and creative. Every wife could make a hobby of nutrition and cooking, preparing appetizing meals designed to keep her family healthy, not just throwing the quickest edible things on the table. Children love to be greeted by the fragrance of homemade bread baking as they arrive home from school. Vegetable gardening is another worthwhile hobby that benefits the whole family. Take time to redecorate unattractive areas of your home and to shop for the best bargains. Visit your neighbors and invite them over for coffee and fellowship around the Bible. Your teaching ability can come in handy there.

If you have a flair for writing or sewing, you can try out these talents while the children are in school. Take a course in a creative craft—decoupage, collage, flower arranging— How about enrolling in a nearby college's foreign-language class?

Don't start all of these things, of course, leaving your family in worse shape than if you were working at a job. But investigate some of them to see what you're missing.

Some husbands don't mind a working wife, but yours does, and pleasing him should be your first consideration. The Scripture says, "Wives, be subject—be submissive and adapt yourselves—to your own husbands as [a service] to the Lord. . . . As the church is subject to Christ, so let wives also be subject in everything to their husbands" (Eph. 5:22, 24 TAB).

If your husband is willing, you may be able to return to your profession someday after the family is out of the nest. Those years of extra time spent with your husband and children will never leave you with regrets. Trust God, yield to your husband, and see what exciting adventures are in store for you.

Enjoying Your Employment

Dear Rita,

I am a working wife, but I don't want to be. My husband insists that I continue my job. I have worked away from home all our married life—about twenty-five years now. There are so many other things I would like to be doing, but I'm stuck in this job. I'm so tired of it. What can I do?

Dear Stuck-in-a-Job,

There are many wives who would like to work but their husbands prefer them not to. Your problem is more unusual.

I believe you should lovingly submit to your husband's wishes and continue to work. Perhaps he feels insecure in his ability to provide for the family adequately without your assistance. Perhaps he is concerned that you will not have enough provision for the years after retirement. Anyway, you've been working a long time, and retirement will not be far away.

The best thing you can do for your husband, for yourself, and your employer is to accept the fact that you are going to work and to enjoy doing it. If you have a bad attitude, it is known by those closest to you. It isn't a good witness to other employees. The only way to get satisfaction out of work that must be done is to do the very best job possible.

Try thanking the Lord that you have a job and that you are physically able to work. Thank the Lord that you chose a husband who would want you to work. Ask God to fulfill whatever plan He has in mind for you on this job. Pray for opportunities to be a joyful witness. Tell your husband how much you are enjoying your job (you will be, you know), and how thankful you are that you can work and that he wants you to. (Have a glass of water ready to revive him if he faints!) When your attitude is right and you're walking according to God's plan for your life, all kinds of interesting things will begin to happen. You may find your husband's ideas beginning to change as he gains more confidence in himself.

Let's look at two women in the New Testament who were in business. One was Lydia, a dealer in purple fabrics. Paul had been directed in a vision to come to the Macedonian area, and on his very first Sabbath in Philippi, he and his companions found a group of women meeting for prayer on the riverbank. I used to think that they had come there to wash their clothes, and that the prayer meeting was an "unofficial" one, but the Greek says that they had a *proseuche** there by the river, a regular place set apart for prayer, so undoubtedly these women had come for that express purpose. Lydia, who was already a worshiper of God, received Jesus and was baptized with her household. It would seem that her home then became the meeting-place for the believers in Philippi (Acts 16:40). This church, which began from a group of women meeting to pray, was, as far as we know, the only one in which Paul found no fault. His letter to this fellowship was written

---

*This word is nearly always equivalent to synagogue. . . . But many consider that the *proseuche* in Acts 16:13, 16 was not a regular synagogue because it was attended only by women. . . . The *proseuche* in our passage may have been an informal meeting place, perhaps in the open air." William F. Arndt and F. Wilbur Gingrich, *A Greek-English Lexicon of the New Testament and Other Early Christian Literature* (Chicago: The University of Chicago Press, 1957) p. 720.

44

after they had been meeting for ten years! We can imagine what a witness Lydia must have been in her business following her conversion.

Priscilla was another working wife (Acts 18:1-3). She and her husband worked together for years in the tent and awning business. Priscilla and her husband, Aquila, met the apostle Paul in Corinth. They had been forced to leave their home in Italy when Claudius issued an edict that all the Jews must leave Rome. Hearing of their plight when he arrived in Corinth, Paul went to see them. It was because of their business—Paul being of the same profession—that he stayed with them. From that time, they worked together off and on, and Priscilla and Aquila traveled with Paul, frequently having a church in their home. They were dear friends throughout Paul's life. What a blessing they received in knowing Paul so closely—all because they had the same profession.

Have you read Proverbs 31, which tells in detail what an ideal wife is like? I think it would be an encouragement to you. One particular portion stands out for you: "She works willingly with her hands" (v. 13b). Don't forget that the Lord wants all that you do to be willingly done, as unto the Lord.

"She is like the merchant's ships; she brings her food from afar. She rises also while it is still night, and gives meat to her household, and a portion to her maidens. She considers a field, and buys it: with the fruit of her hands she plants a vineyard. She girds her loins with strength, and strengthens her arms. She sees that her merchandise is good: her candle doesn't go out at night. . . . She makes fine linen, and sells it; and delivers girdles to the merchant. . . . She looks well to the ways of her household, and eats not the bread of idleness" (Prov. 31:14-18, 24, 27). These verses make this woman sound like quite a businesswoman, don't they? She was certainly what we would term a working wife today. Look at the blessings she received!

"Her children rise up, and call her blessed; her husband also, and he praises her. Many daughters have done virtuously [the Hebrew says "have gotten rich"] but you excel them all. Favour is deceitful, and beauty is vain: but a woman that fears the Lord, she shall be praised. Give her of the fruit of her hands; and let her own works praise her in the gates" (Prov. 31:28-31).

Don't consider yourself "stuck in a job" anymore, but accept the fact that God has permitted you to be placed there, and thank Him.

Taking the whole armor of God.

Wife-Swapping

Dear Rita,

My husband isn't "with it" anymore as far as Christianity goes. We are still running with the same friends we used to before we became Christians. Usually there is heavy drinking at our parties and some are now even wife-swapping. I feel sure my husband would even like to get us involved in this, if I would consent, but I'm not interested in the wife- and husband-swapping bit. What advice could you give me? I don't have the blessings I once experienced with the Lord Jesus, especially right after I was baptized with the Holy Spirit. Can you tell me why?

Dear Not-Interested,

It's a good thing you're *not* (interested, that is!), but shouldn't you feel more strongly against this kind of degrading activity? Could it be that the influence of the world from these "friends" has slowly begun to seep back into your life, so that your new life in Christ is being stifled? The more a Christian exposes his mind to the thinking of unregenerated lost humanity—through constant fellowship, reading the latest shady novel, or watching the television without discrimination—the more the presence and fellowship of the Lord Jesus is going to diminish, until that person begins to wonder if he or she ever knew God in the first place.

Satan is a thief and a robber, and he is busily trying to rob you and your husband of the most precious gift in this life—fellowship with God Almighty. You can stop this from happening. Tell your husband if there is wife-swapping going on, you refuse to be a party to this kind of abominable activity. Meanwhile, remember to go the extra mile in submitting to your husband in areas that are not wrong.

When the Bible speaks of a wife being submitted to her husband, God does not intend that to be taken so literally as to require her to participate in immoral activity. We are to be submitted only in those areas that agree with God's standards. Ephesians, chapter five, certainly teaches the wife to be submitted to her husband, but you cannot submit to a husband "as unto the Lord" if he is acting like a pagan and wanting you to act like one.*

Partner exchanging is wrong. God's pattern from the beginning of creation was one man for one woman. Hear what the Scripture says: "Do you not know that your bodies are the members of Christ? Shall I then take the members of Christ, and make them the members of a harlot? God forbid. What? Do you not know that the one who joins himself to a harlot [prostitute] is one body? For two, He says, shall be one flesh. . . . *Flee* fornication. . . . He that commits fornication sins against his own body. What? Do you not know that your body is the temple of the Holy Ghost which is in you, which you

---

*For a fuller treatment of the subject of submission read "*Dear Deld-Back*," pp. 123-126.

have of God, and you are not your own? For you are bought with a price: therefore glorify God in your body, and in your spirit, which are God's" (I Cor. 6:15-16; 18-20).

There is nothing Satan likes to do more than to defile the temples of the Holy Spirit (Christians). A temple is a place of worship, and this is what our bodies are supposed to be—places of constant fellowship with, and worship to God. Even as Jesus Himself had to cast the thieves out of His Father's temple, so we may have to cast away the works of the enemy from our lives, so God's presence can once again fill us.

If you find you must go to some of the parties with your husband (without swapping anything), then go wearing the whole armor of God, and have some solid Christians in prayer for you during this time. Also, remember temperance or self-control is a fruit of the Holy Spirit. Keep your mind clear and unfogged (stay sober), so God can work through you. Philippians 4:5 says, "Let your moderation be known to all men. The Lord is at hand."

Get some good charismatic Christian fellowship once or twice a week. "What," you may ask, "is a charismatic Christian?" Charismata is the Greek word meaning,"gifts of God's grace" or "gifts of God's love." The most concise listing of God's gifts for today is found in I Corinthians 12:8-10. They are: the word of wisdom, the word of knowledge, discerning of spirits, gifts of faith, working of miracles, gifts of healing, prophecy, various kinds of tongues, interpretation of tongues. A charismatic Christian then, in the broader sense, is any Christian who believes these gifts are available to the Body of Christ on earth and is open for any of them to be manifest in his or her life.

In the more specific sense, the term "charismatic" is used of those who have received the Baptism in the Holy Spirit spoken of by the Lord Jesus Christ in Acts 1, and experienced by the first believers on the Day of Pentecost. This Baptism, or outflowing, of the Holy Spirit, from where He dwells in the innermost being of every believer, to baptize, or inundate, soul and body, results in a far greater awareness of the Holy Spirit and His work, and a fuller manifestation of the charismatic gifts. (For an in-depth study of the gifts of the Holy Spirit, see *The Holy Spirit and You.**)

Pray with the Spirit and with your understanding also, and read the Scriptures daily. Get some good Spirit-filled tapes and listen to them while you iron clothes or work around the kitchen or drive to the grocery store. If you do these things, you will not only once again know the presence of God, but your life itself will begin to have an unspoken influence on your husband and even on the people at the parties you attend. They will feel the presence of Christ in you. If these friends don't change, ask God to give you and your husband some new ones. If you follow the preceding advice, I believe many of your present

*See p. 6 for full citation in a footnote.

friends will soon be asking you to tell them what has made the difference in your life.

Husband Who Can Cook!

Dear Rita,

Do you think it is unmasculine for a man to cook or help in the kitchen? My husband likes to cook a meal once in a while as a surprise for me, but a friend says I'm wrong scripturally to let him do a woman's work.

Dear Fortunate Wife,

How nice to have such a considerate husband! Although the kitchen is primarily the domain of the wife, I see nothing wrong with the husband choosing to cook or help with the dishes on occasion. I feel sorry for men who have never learned to do anything but boil water. They are helpless when left by themselves and have to rely entirely on restaurant food. It's just good common sense to know some of the basics of cooking.

Jesus was the best example of masculinity that ever existed. After His resurrection, He prepared a meal of grilled fish and fresh bread to feed the disciples following their fishing trip. His manliness wasn't threatened by this. Indeed, isn't it possible that Mary, His mother, might have given Him some cooking lessons while He was growing up?!

Just before His death and resurrection, Jesus shared a meal with His disciples. We call this the Last Supper, and it was the traditional Passover Feast, made up of unleavened bread, lamb roast, a salad mixture of crushed apples, nuts and raisins, bitter herbs, greens or parsley, hard-boiled eggs, whole red apples, and wine, according to Ruth Specter, in *The Bud and Flower of Judaism* (Springfield, Mo.: Gospel Publishing House, 1955). The place where they met would have had to be well cleaned from top to bottom to make sure there was no speck of leaven, which symbolized sin. Jesus directed Peter and John to make preparation for the feast, and it certainly sounds as though they did the cooking and cleaning themselves (Luke 22:8, 12, 13).

After escaping from Jezebel, Elijah was sleeping in the wilderness. He was awakened by an angel who provided him with a freshly baked cake and a jar of water and told him to eat. From the context, it sounds as if the angel had just prepared the "cake baked on the coals" which Elijah saw (I Kings 19:6). In the Bible, angels were not females as in popular religious art, but strong, masculine beings. The cake was so nutritious that after Elijah had slept and eaten again, he was able to journey forty days and nights with no other food. (The angel's cake must have been very nutritious! Wish I had the recipe.)

Seriously, I do not like to see the exchanging of roles—in which the husband stays at home and does all the housework, cooking, and caring for the children while the wife goes out to work. This could be very confusing to children and might cause them some psychological harm. Also, being carried to extremes, this reversal of traditional roles could, in time, be harmful to the marriage itself.

In some situations, equal sharing in household work and caring for children is necessary—as when the husband is in school and the wife is working to help him complete his education. This, however, should be adjusted to a more normal pattern as soon as the education is completed. Of course, there are cases where the husband may be ill and unable to work; in such instances, the wife might have to continue working away from home. Also, if the wife is ill, the husband might shoulder more than the usual household responsibilities.

You, I repeat, are fortunate to have such a thoughtful husband. Tell your friend that you are so submitted to your husband that you wouldn't think of ordering him out of his own kitchen. And pray for her, as she perhaps has not been so blessed.

The Latter Married Years

Dear Rita,

My husband and I have had twenty-two years of happy married life. Now our youngest child has entered college and we are without any children at home. Lately I've been thinking about old age and what it will do to our marriage. No relationship can remain stationary, but the thoughts of our life together in the future and what it will be like concern me.

Dear Concerned,

The story of the marriage in Cana has for a long time been a favorite of mine. You no doubt know it. Remember when the party ran out of wine? Jesus came to the rescue by turning the six jars of water into wine. Normally, the last wine to be served is of the poorest quality, but the wine Jesus created at the end of the feast was the best of all (John 2:1-11).

Often I have used this analogy to illustrate the work of the Holy Spirit, but recently I heard a Lutheran minister put it another way. My husband and I were invited to a wedding of two young friends. The minister's talk to them was taken from this story. He said, in effect, "Some people regard the first years of marriage as the special ones and expect things to degenerate as time goes on. But as the Scripture says, The best wine at the marriage feast was saved for last, so also I believe that in a Christ-centered marriage, God also saves the best for last!" And, may I add, wine does grow better with age.

The miracle at the wedding in Cana, the beginning of Jesus' ministry on earth, was a very important occasion. I think the Scripture story is an analogy of Jesus' spiritual union with the bride of Christ, the Church, assuring that our love and fellowship with Him will grow better and better. Since all marriage should be patterned after Jesus' marriage to His bride, you should confidently expect that yours, too, will keep getting better.

When you first received Jesus into your life, it was wonderful, wasn't it? Is it any less wonderful now than it was at first? Will it get even better? Of course it will. Your marriage, then, is a picture of something infinitely greater which is yet to come.

You've had twenty-two years to adjust to one person, and I imagine there were many rough edges worn off both of your lives. You've had many joys and sorrows. There are beautiful memories. The two of you have become very close in spirit, soul, and body. You often think and speak as one. With this kind of unity, what a team you should be, and better with every passing day.

I'm tithing my time to God. What do you think He would have me do around here for 2½ hours?

Tithing

Dear Rita,

My husband is a throw-a-dollar-in-the-plate nominal kind of Christian. Right now, there is conflict in our home because I believe in and have been tithing.* I maintain that the money is the Lord's, while my husband says that it is his money. He says by tithing our income, I am hampering his efforts to save for retirement. I'm in a quandary to know what to do!

Dear In-a-Quandary,

The Scripture certainly supports you in your desire to tithe. It may be annoying for you when your husband asserts that it's *his* money. "After all," you may think, "I work hard at home to make it possible for him to go out and earn the money."

However, the eternal viewpoint is better; you are so right in saying the money is the Lord's. Even when we tithe, we are giving back to the Lord only that which is already *His*. We brought nothing into this world, and we'll take nothing out of it except those riches we let God store in our lives and in our

---

*Tithing means giving ten percent off the top of your income to your church; *offerings* to your church or other places are over and above this amount. The tithe was an Old Testament rule. Since New Testament times, we should realize that 100 percent of all we have belongs to God; however, the tithe is still a good basic minimum standard of giving today.

heavenly bank account (I Cor. 3:12-15; Matt. 6:19-21). The Scripture says, "All things come of Thee, and of Thine own have we given Thee" (I Chron. 29:14b). Since this is true, there is nothing we can actually give the Lord but our love, and this is what He wants most of all.

I can see why you are in a quandary. In fact, you are in the middle of a paradox: the Scripture teaches tithing, and it also teaches the wife to be submissive to her husband. In your situation, you can't do both but must choose one or the other. Let me ask you this question: Which is most important—to be right (which you are) and to force your husband to continue to tithe, or to submit to his decision, have a peaceful home, and by your loving attitude lead your husband to a vital and living relationship with Jesus?

Jesus scolded the Scribes and Pharisees because after having been so correct in tithing, even to meticulously giving ten percent of their spices—"mint, anise, and cummin"—they omitted the most important things in the law—love, mercy, faith, and judgment* (Matt. 23:23; Luke 11:42).

It is my belief that you should obey your husband in this matter. As you do so, be careful not to do it with a judgmental attitude, however, but with great love. After all, God wants your husband's soul, not his money. When your husband truly gives his

---

*The Jew saw the word "judgment" not in a condemnatory kind of sitting in judgment, but in the positive sense of doing things properly, or knowing the right thing to do in every situation.

heart to God, and especially when he becomes a charismatic Christian, he will want to tithe. The new wine of Pentecost has a way of liberating the pocketbook!

In the meantime, be sure you are taking an interest in planning for your husband's retirement. Let him know of your genuine concern. Read some good books on this subject. One is *How to Serve God in Retirement*, by Paul W. Travis, published by The Foundation Press, Santa Ana, California.

Retirement is a difficult transition period for many men, and they may begin to feel very insecure and helpless. This is when your role as a helpmate could be most needed, and may be when he finally has time to sit down and evaluate his life and decide it is time for a closer walk with God. Retirement can be the best time of your life together, if you keep that sweet and helpful attitude.

While you are waiting for God's moving in your husband's life and pocketbook, you might be able to do some part-time work and tithe from this, if your husband is agreeable. I would not recommend tithing from your grocery or household money, as this would not be submission and would cause more problems when it was discovered.

Your tithing wouldn't always have to be in dollars and cents. Tithe some of your *time* in praying for your pastor, his family, and church members in need, or in helping in the church office, book or tape library. Be expecting God to show you some creative ways to give to your church. God is your real source of supply, and that supply is unlimited.

Happy tithing!

HEADSHIP

Passive Man

Dear Rita,

My husband is inclined to be a passive person, whereas I am strong and definite. Because of this, I have tended to be the leader in our family. Recently God has shown me my mistake of domineering in our home, and I am making every effort to correct it. It is not easy, because my husband has found the passive role requires much less effort. My children lack respect for their father as a result of my former attitude, and regaining authority with them does not come easy. I'm thankful that I realized what was taking place in our home before it was too late.

What will happen to our society if men become more and more passive and continue to relinquish their roles as leaders and heads of the family?

Dear Not-Too-Late,

The third chapter of the Book of Isaiah is highly relevant today. It says, "I will give children to be their princes, and babes shall rule over them. . . . The child shall behave himself proudly against the ancient. . . . As for my people, children are their oppressors, and women rule over them. O my people, they which lead you cause you to err, and destroy the way of your paths" (Isa. 3:4, 5b,12).

This is certainly a picture of what is happening in our society. We are reaping the results of such things as "progressive education" today, when we see the undisciplined lives of so many young people. Also, respect for parents and adults in general is sadly lacking on the whole. Many youths order their parents around, and family life is often "hellish."

There are some good things that the "libbers," the feminists of today, are working to achieve, such as: equal property rights and credit ratings, equal job opportunity and equal pay, recognition for the work women have done instead of using them as ghost writers or researchers where men get the credit, and so forth. However, when they teach that a woman who enjoys being a homemaker cannot find her real fulfillment there, they are wrong. When "libbers" say that we must put all the infants and small children into nurseries, and get out there and compete with the men, they are fighting God's plan. When "libbers" encourage women to fight for wholesale abortion, and say, "There are no roles in life that ought to be restricted to either men or women,"* they are helping to head our civilization to its ruin.

As women move into the roles of the men, the men will withdraw more and more. As the men withdraw from leadership in the family unit, the wives and children lose respect and love for them. Husbands who don't know God's plan and/or are just too tired and passive to resist, are selling out.

---

*Lucy Komisar, "A Feminist Manifesto," *Reader's Digest*, August 1971, p. 105.

Perversion of all kinds can be traced to identity loss and exchanged roles in the home.

Some people also feel that the unisex idea being pushed in the free world has been planned by those who would like to see its destruction. Changing the accepted male and female roles is a large step toward the breakdown of our society.

If men don't take their places as leaders under God, the family unit will decay, divorce will increase, and marriage as we know it today will begin to disappear. As these things occur, immorality and perversion will grow. God's hand of protection over us will be removed, and we will come under the rule of despotic and demonic powers. Thomas Jefferson said, "If men will not be ruled by God, they will be ruled by tyrants." There is a choice to be made.

We must work against these things taking over our culture. More women should do as you have done, stepping back to make room for the men to move forward into their proper roles. Let's help our men to be men.

I'm so glad that you're not too late. I trust you'll help open the eyes of other women to what they can do to curb the tide of evil. The Scripture says, "When the enemy shall come in like a flood, the Spirit of the Lord shall lift up a standard against him"(Isa. 59:19b). Let us cooperate with the Holy Spirit to lift the standard high.

Women's Lib

Dear Rita,

What is the reason for the big "put down" on women? Why is it that women have been in subservient positions throughout history? Who's to blame?

Through the news on T.V. and radio, and in reading the newspaper and magazines on the subject of women's rights, I've learned such things as the following: In Africa, even today, the bride is paid for as a common chattel. Muslim mosques have signs that say: "Women and dogs and other impure animals not permitted." In the Mohammedan belief, a woman is on such a low level, she is thought not to have an eternal soul. Four wives are allowed each Mohammedan male, even today. Orthodox Jewish men still say this morning prayer: "Blessed art thou, O Lord our God, King of the Universe, who has not made me a woman." In India, congratulations are not given to parents unless the new arrival is a boy. In Japan, women are served their meals after the men have been served, and women may board trains only after all the men have boarded. "While the Japanese government has ratified an international 'equal remuneration' resolution, Japanese women are still suffering pocketbook discrimination and are paid an average of roughly 50 percent less than men."* Even in the U.S.A., women have been allowed the right to vote only since 1920, and in seven other countries today, they are barred from voting in the national elections. The list of prejudices against women in many Christian denominations is too long to go into. I have experienced discrimination in my own church.

All this is getting my dander up. Since listening to and reading recent reports, I'm getting less and less enamored with my life of being chained to this house and our kids.

Dear Put-Down,

In our society today, almost everyone is blaming someone else for their problems. The institutionalized Church blames the world, and the world blames the Church. Young blame the old, and the old blame the young. The ecologists blame industry, and industry blames ecology. The different nations and races continue to blame one another. Women blame men, and men blame women.

Who really is to blame?

We must go back to the beginning of mankind in order to truly see where all this misery started. The story of the first man and woman contains spiritual truths that are foundational for the rest of the Scripture. Eve was asked a leading question by Satan, starting with, "Has God said . . .?" implant-

*Beverly Ann Deepe, "The Women's Lib Movement Around the World," *Clipper Magazine*, October 1971, p. 9.

ing the first doubt in her mind about God's goodness and honesty. The enemy went on to imply that God was holding out on His creatures, and that His plan was not in their best interests. The enemy is a smooth talker, and Eve believed his lies rather than God's words. The woman was the first to fall into the trap, and the man followed.* They didn't trust God.

As He was sentencing the serpent/Satan for his part in the fall of man, God said, "And I will put enmity between thee and the woman, and between thy seed and her seed: he shall bruise thy head [a fatal wound] and thou shalt bruise his heal [temporary wound]" (Gen. 3:15 ASV).

Enmity means "a deep-seated hatred." Satan especially hated the woman. She had exposed his trickery (she told on him) and although her gullibility had delivered to him the dominion over this world which had been given to Adam and Eve, yet his rule would now be limited. Through the woman's Seed (Jesus), Satan's doom and the breaking of his dominion were assured.

The woman, of course, tried to put all the blame on Satan. She was very angry with him, because originally she was to have shared dominion with the man in ruling the earth. "And God said, Let us make

---

*For a book of Christian fiction that carries out an imagined temptation of the first woman on another planet, read *Perelandra* by C.S. Lewis (New York, N.Y.: Macmillan, 1968). Dr. Lewis does a marvelous job of enacting an original temptation scene, and through this, not only shows us what the first temptation could have been like, but reveals to us how the enemy continues to work today.

man in our image, after our likeness: and let *them* [Adam and Eve] *have dominion* over the fish of the sea, and over the fowl of the air, and over the cattle, and *over all the earth*, and over every creeping thing that creepeth upon the earth" (Gen. 1:26). Now, neither one would have dominion (for a time), and the woman would be ruled over by man and also bear children with much pain.* The one hope she had was that a woman would give birth to a Man-Child who would defeat the enemy, and save her and all others who would trust in Him—Jesus the Messiah.

The hatred Satan has for the woman has been proved throughout history again and again. Most women sense they have an enemy, but they don't really know who he is. When a soldier is on a battlefield, the greatest danger is in not knowing who or where the enemy is. Unless women come alive in Christ Jesus, thereby receiving spiritual understanding, they will think it's men alone who are oppressing them. Satan, of course, works through those (men *and* women) who are under his control, but when a woman knows the source of the malice aimed at her, she can, through Jesus, have victory.

I believe Jesus is in favor of women having equal educational opportunities, equal pay according to ability, the right to be treated as intelligent human beings, the right to vote, and the right to share teaching, gifts, and talents with the Body of

---

*The woman was always, from the very first, created to be a "helpmate" to her husband, and this role has never been changed. A "help meet," as the KJV puts it, is one who "walks alongside of," and supports.

Christ. The way Jesus treated women, as recorded in the Gospels, shows that He never pushed them down, but always lifted them up. Mary, the mother of Jesus, says it this way: "For He hath regarded the *low estate of His handmaiden:* for, behold, from henceforth all generations shall call me blessed" (Luke 1:48). God the Father has regarded or considered the low estate of women in general throughout the ages, and through His Son has delighted in lifting them back up into the position He originally intended for them. In fact, the position is infinitely better for both men and women now than at the beginning, because we were then only His creatures and now we are His children. God always makes something better out of our mistakes if we will only repent and turn them over to Him.

Christian women who are walking in the Spirit have been restored equal dominion over this earth. Through Jesus, they have authority over Satan and his kingdom of darkness. Jesus said, "Truly truly I tell you, the [one] believing in me, the works which I do that one also will do and greater [than] these he will do" (John 14:12 NGT).* The Christian woman should expect to have much authority in Jesus. She may be used to command sickness and disease to depart, to cast out evil spirits, to set the oppressed free, to raise the dead, and to command the wind and waves to obey her. If she is in danger, she may escape from those who would seek to do her bodily

*In the first part of this verse, the impersonal gender is used. In the second half, "he" means both genders.

injury; she may command a charging wild animal to be still.

I read an article some time ago which told of a woman who was forced into a car by two men, but as she called upon the name of Jesus for help, she was released at the next stoplight. One of the persons in Indonesia who has been used by God to raise the dead is a woman.**

After I was baptized in the Holy Spirit, I was told to be sure always to have a man pray with anyone who needed deliverance, because "the woman was the weaker vessel" (I Pet. 3:7).* When the Lord presented me with the first person who needed deliverance prayer—prayer to cast out the evil spirits that were tormenting her—I didn't have time to run and get a man, an ordained minister, or anyone else. The woman needed help then and there; in her wild state, there was no time to waste. It's so wonderful to know that Jesus sets people free, and He will use any channel who is open to Him. A tremendous number of women today are also being used to heal the sick in Jesus' Name.

It is true that there are some extreme teachings going 'round about women's ministry, just as there

---

**John Meyers, "Indonesia: The Greatest Work of God in the World Today," *Acts Magazine*, vol. I, no. 3, p. 10.

*The "weaker vessel" here obviously doesn't mean "less intelligent." It could be referring to a couple of things: that the woman was weaker as far as the original temptation was concerned, and also that the woman is not as muscular or strong physically. Physical strength was no doubt what my friend was concerned about, but spiritual strength is what matters in such situations.

are about many other things. Some even teach that since the husband is the "lord" of the wife, she cannot hear from God except through her husband. Jesus wants women liberated from such ideas, so that they will realize that they, too, can be used in miraculous ways to express His mighty love and power through their lives. He doesn't want His work through them hindered by the idea that they are "mere women."

On the other hand, even though women who are in Christ are given back their dominion in the world, woman was originally created as man's "help-meet." Man became the ruler over his wife by reason of the Fall. Yet a Christian husband does not "rule" his wife, but receives her again as a "help-meet," and together they share dominion over the creation.

Some have tried to make it seem that the only directive in the Scripture is that the woman should "submit" to her husband, but Paul also says that we should "submit ourselves one to another in the fear of God" (Eph. 5:21-22). This speaks to husbands and wives as well; submission is a Christian principle. A major Greek lexicon defines submission as "voluntary yielding in love."*

The idea of male and female equality is not new, but God's own standard expressed through Jesus Christ. Jesus didn't come to give His life only for

*William F. Arndt and F. Wilbur Gingrich, *A Greek-English Lexicon of the New Testament and Other Early Christian Literature* (Chicago: The University of Chicago Press, 1957) p. 855.

men to be saved, but for men and women, girls and boys. God's children are equally precious in His sight and can bring their needs to Him in prayer at any time or any place. Each person will appear before God individually responsible for his or her actions in this life.

I hope and pray that your life as a Christian wife and mother will become more and more meaningful to you. This is your first and most important ministry. The shaping of young lives is an awesome responsibility and also can be extremely rewarding for you.

Ask yourself if the women's lib types you have seen in the news are really happy and fulfilled? I know that it's important to keep up with the basic news of the day, but to constantly immerse yourself in it is unhealthy. Any T.V. or radio program that makes you feel "put down" should be shut off. Pray for God to mold you into the most beautiful wife and mother possible, one filled with *His* power and *His* authority.

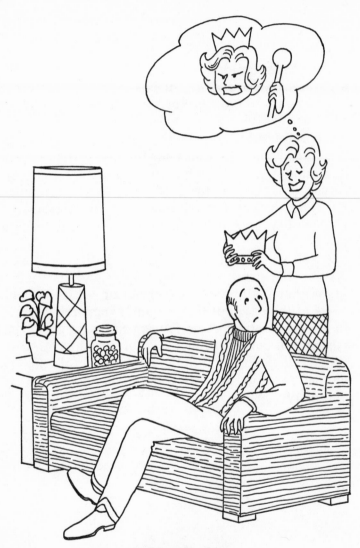

**Hold still, dear;
this isn't going to hurt at all.**

God Looks at Hearts

Dear Rita,

There is a lot of emphasis on submitted wives today, but in listening to some of the gals, I seem to hear them saying that obeying your husband is really a way to get him obligated to you so that you can get him to do what you want him to. "Be sweet and submissive, and you can twist him around your little finger." Do you think this is an honest motivation for being a good wife? Is it a Christian idea?

Dear Desiring-Honest-Motivation,

I think you've put your finger on a very subtle deception. If the enemy can get women to practice submission with an ulterior motive, then he can cancel out any real good coming from it. The motive for being submitted should not be for the woman to get her own way.

Because of their historic subservient role, many women have become master manipulators. Christian women need to be on guard against old fallen habit patterns which would urge them to get their way by falling back into manipulative techniques under the guise of submission. Of such women, Aristotle said in 330 B.C., "What difference does it make whether women rule or the rulers are ruled by the women?" If a woman practices secret rule, she may be instrumental in causing her husband to fall short of God's best plan for his life.

The most important thing for the woman to consider is that the Lord sees what she is doing and her heart's motivation. A Scripture in I Samuel appropriately says, "The Lord sees not as man sees; for man looks on the outward appearance, but the Lord looks on the heart" (I Sam. 16:7b). A woman should ask herself, "Do I want my own selfish way, or do I want the Lord's blessing?" The two do not go together.

When Jesus proclaimed what we sometimes call the golden rule, He didn't say, "If you are good to others, they will be good to you." He said, "Whatever you wish that men would do to you, do so to them" (Matt. 7:12a RSV). They may then proceed to mistreat you, but your job is to continue to treat them as you would like to be treated.

In marriage, obeying your husband is not a *method* for getting him to treat you well or to do what you want him to; it is just the way God wants you to treat your husband. It may not result in his reformation (if he needs it) or his being especially good to you. It isn't a *method* at all, but *obedience* to God's law of love. God doesn't indicate that you'll get your way by being nice; the important thing is that you'll be pleasing Him.

Jealous Husband

Dear Rita,

I keep hearing women talking about being submissive to their husbands, but I'm afraid of being a submissive wife. My husband, John, is so jealous, that if he had his way, I'd never even be able to call my own sister. Sometimes he storms through the house, slamming doors and even throws the first thing that can be broken, such as a lamp, a dish, and so forth. I want to do what's right, yet I don't want to end up with a life that is so constricted I can't even talk to my own relatives. What exactly does Scripture mean when it says for women to be submissive to their husbands?

Dear Afraid,

To be submissive to your husband, in the Christian sense of the word, is to be voluntarily obedient to him in your own love and in the love of Jesus—as long as what he is asking you to do is not at odds with what God directs in the Scriptures.

Take time to prayerfully evaluate the reason for your husband's jealousy. Has he always been this way, or is this a fairly recent occurrence? What reasons can you think of for his actions? Is there anything on your part which helped to bring this about? If there is, you will need to prove yourself. Walls that have been built up take a little effort and time to tear down. Seriously work on trying to regain his confidence and trust. A flirtatious attitude around other men—even if it's in jesting—may keep a husband feeling insecure in his wife's love, besides being unhealthy for everyone involved.

If his jealousy is an unrealistic quirk, perhaps a hangover from his childhood, your husband, of course, needs help, but he will have to come to this realization himself. If he is an intelligent man, and I am sure he is, he may be led to realize that his behavior is exaggerated, and come to seek help from a capable counselor.* If he is genuinely unable to control his jealous reactions, even though he knows rationally they are out of line with the circumstances, he may need prayer for deliverance. Many Christians grow uneasy when deliverance is talked about, because of some extreme teachings that are going the rounds today, but long experience in prayer and counseling leaves no doubt that Christians may be so bound in their psychological natures (mind, emotions, will) that they need special prayer help to get free. If your husband recognizes such a need, then perhaps you and another friend might pray with him. Even if he does not, you can pray privately that he will be released from the enemy's oppression. For more on this, see our book, *The Holy Spirit and You*, pages 148-154.

No matter which situation fits your particular case, avoid doing the things that annoy your hus-

---

*A helpful book on Christian counseling is *Competent to Counsel* by Jay E. Adams, (Nutley, New Jersey: Presbyterian and Reformed Publishing Co., 1971).

band when he is at home. Ask your sister to telephone you during the day. Try to develop good will between your husband and your relatives. Build him up in their eyes, and don't divulge family secrets. Perhaps you could encourage some of your relatives to call up specifically to speak to your husband from time to time, taking an interest in him, too, so he won't feel left out.

One of the greatest prayer groups is that composed of a Christian husband and wife. Ecclesiastes says: "Two are better than one; because they have a good reward for their labour. For if they fall, the one will lift up his fellow. . . . And if one prevail against him, two shall withstand him; and a threefold cord [husband, wife, and Jesus] is not quickly broken" (4:9-10a,12). Another Scripture says: "One shall put a thousand to flight, but two shall put ten thousand to flight." If your husband is willing for you to pray directly with him, this is very effective, as the preceding verses also declare. You might begin by finding something in your own life that you could ask him to pray for.

My husband, Dennis, and I have prayed for one another's needs ever since we were married and have seen great results both spiritually and in natural ways as a direct result. I can highly recommend this. Praying with your mate is so very effective since you're completely committed to one another, and therefore you can be totally honest.*

---

*A single person can also find a prayer partner for this kind of help. It should be a person of the same sex who is established in the Lord and one who has been proven to keep confidences.

As you continue to pray about these difficulties, God will direct you and give you the strength and understanding needed.

Head Covering

Dear Rita,

I think it's important for us to study all Scriptures in the Bible pertaining to women so that we may quickly learn these particular lessons God has for us. I have puzzled over Paul's letter to the Corinthians and wonder just what was meant by the head covering for the woman and why it isn't practiced in many churches today. Can you help me?

Dear Puzzled,

This is a difficult topic, and people have varying opinions.

Let's look at some of the basic Scriptures on the subject. "Every man who has something on his head while praying or prophesying, disgraces his head. But every woman who has her head uncovered while praying or prophesying, disgraces her head; for she is one and the same with her whose head is shaved. For if a woman does not cover her head, let her also have her hair cut off; but if it is disgraceful for a woman to have her hair cut off or her head shaved, let her cover her head. For a man ought not to have his head covered, since he is the image and glory of God; but the woman is the glory of man. For man does not originate from woman, but woman from man: for indeed man was not created for the woman's sake, but woman for the man's sake. Therefore the woman ought to have a symbol of authority on her head, because of the angels. However, in the Lord, neither is woman independent of man, nor is man independent of woman. For as the woman originates from the man, so also the man has his birth through the woman; and all things originate from God. Judge for yourselves: is it proper for a woman to pray to God with head uncovered? Does not even nature itself teach you that if a man has long hair, it is a dishonor to him, but if a woman has long hair, it is a glory to her? For her hair is given to her for a covering" (I Cor. 11:4-15 NASB).

To the Corinthians, Paul's letter may have been intended as a reproof to both sexes for falling into a style of manners which confused the sexes and would eventually have had a bad influence morally and psychologically. Perhaps some of the men were letting their hair grow extra long and were also wearing the tallith (fringe) or head covering. Many of the women, on the other hand, feeling liberated, may have decided to cut off their long hair and to discard their head coverings entirely. At first glance, it might have been hard to tell the men from the women!

Now for some background on the above statements. The Romans and Egyptians in ancient times permitted their hair and beards to grow long; even Hebrew men such as Samson and those taking Nazirite vows did so. However, about three centuries before the Christian era, men in the Roman culture began to wear their hair fairly short or just over the ears. (The pictures of Jesus with very long hair are probably not accurate.) This practice must have been quite general in the Gospel Age—at least wherever Paul traveled, it must have been so, since he refers to it as an acknowledged and nearly universal fact (I Cor. 11:14-15).

The Hebrew men in ancient times also used to wear a fringed or tasseled outer garment; it was an oblong garment with a hole in the center through which to put the head. This garment was modified and made smaller and is now called the tallith or cover. It is worn by every married Jewish Orthodox man at morning prayers; it covers the head to show respect to God.* Men in Orthodox synagogues today wear a yarmulke, a little skullcap, to cover their heads.

Perhaps these comparatively modern Jewish traditions were just getting their start at this time.

---

*John McClintock and James Strong, Cyclopedia of Biblical, Theological and Ecclesiastical Literature (Grand Rapids, Michigan: Baker Book House, 1969), vol. III, p. 678 and vol. IV, p. 24.

The only Hebrew who wore a head covering for worship in the Old Testament was the high priest, as part of his garments worn into the Holy of Holies. Paul was against these "modern" practices and pointed out that men were first in the order of creation, and since they had headship under Christ, they should not relinquish their place of authority by covering their heads in church. If a man were to do so, it would be a shame to him, and would also dishonor Jesus, His Head.

Paul reasons with the women next. He speaks to them in terms of the accepted customs of the day. "In those days modest, respectable women didn't appear in public without their heads covered. Only women without proper self-respect, or women of bad reputation, broke this custom."* Paul says that if the women uncover their heads in church, it will look as though they have bad morals—as if they had been caught in adultery and had their hair cut off or their heads shaved.

"Libertines of the church may have argued that the Christian woman is freed from the unwritten laws of society and of all places should be able to express this freedom in church. But Paul reasons that women should not come before God in a manner considered indecent elsewhere."** For women to have departed from the general practice of the countries where they resided would have brought

*Charles M. Laymon, ed., The Interpreter's One-Volume Commentary on the Bible (New York, N.Y.: Abingdon, 1971), pp. 805-806.

**Ibid., p. 806.

reproach on the Christian name, a dishonor to themselves and their husbands.

"Paul conceives the head covering to be a sign of exercising delegated authority under man. He probably had in mind the root-connection between the Hebrew terms for covering (*radid*), and submission (*radad*). Even though the woman had long hair which was a natural covering, yet the wearing of an additional covering over her own hair showed that she of her own will had chosen to wear a token of her inner submission."*

What is all this saying to the Christian woman today? We know that customs are different now and that an unveiled woman in church doesn't automatically mean one unsubmissive to authority. In fact, a woman could wear a head covering in church for show and be rebellious in her heart against her husband and all other authorities over her. Perhaps it's something like this. If it were to become a custom for all atheists to wear red and pink shirts or blouses, it would be natural for your minister to warn you against wearing them. However, years later, when that apparel was no longer a badge of atheism, Christians might in good conscience wear it.

In the Episcopal, Anglican, Roman Catholic, and some other historic churches, women today may still wear head coverings such as the mantilla,

*R. Jamiseon, Fausset, and Brown, eds., *Commentary on the Whole Bible* (Grand Rapids, Mich.: Zondervan, 1962), pp. 1211-1212.

chapel cap, head scarf, kerchief, hats, and so forth, although this tradition is today being given less emphasis in many churches where it used to be required.

Jesus, in the Gospels, did not teach on the subject of head coverings, although He certainly taught by word and deed both submission and humility. The woman's greatest covering (protection) is that inner submission to the Lord Jesus and therefore to her husband and to all other authorities over her. A spiritual principle here is that she should *not* minister in prayer or prophecy or any of the other gifts if she is not submitted. Submission is a shield of protection against Satan's devices. When a woman walks in divine order, she can move in greater freedom in spiritual things. If a head covering reminds her of her God-ordained role, then it has served a good purpose.

It says, "As unto the Lord,"
not "As the Lord."

Worship God, Not Man

Dear Rita,

　With all the teaching on wives being submitted to their husbands, isn't there, on the other side of the picture, a danger of women being taught to worship their husbands instead of God? I am certainly in favor of women submitting to their own husbands, but against husband worship.

Dear Non-Husband-Worshiper,

　In every teaching, we must guard against extremes and aim for a balanced viewpoint. Although the overly submissive wife is rarer than the under-submissive one, both are distortions of what God desires.

　Your question brings to mind a conversation I had with a woman in California recently. Her story went something like this:

　"When I hear teaching on submission of the wife to the husband, I have a different picture than most American women. In my youth, I remember my father as a little dictator who kept my mother and us children completely under his thumb. My mother seemed to worship my father rather than God. As a consequence, when I was married, I had no problem being submissive, but I had other problems: that of not knowing my own self as a person and being afraid to make any necessary decisions

I was fortunate to marry a man just the opposite of my father, one who wanted me to develop my talents and abilities as a person, and not simply be an appendage of himself. My husband respected my opinions and talked things over with me before making major decisions. Because of his love and consideration, we had a very beautiful married life, and after my husband died, I had the strength to go on living. Being on my own, I had to look for a job and found one as a dishwasher for a large hospital. Due to the confidence my husband had helped instill in me, within a few years' time, I rose from dishwasher to supervisor. My job requires constant decision making."

Let us look at a few of the Scriptures which have led some to teach husband worship:

Ephesians 5:33 says, "Let . . . the wife see that she reverence her husband." The word "reverence" indicates "worship" to us today, but a more accurate word in keeping with the teaching of the whole of Scripture would be "respect." A free translation of the Greek would say it like this: "The wife is supposed to respect her man."

First Corinthians 11:7 says, "Man . . . is the image and glory of God: but the woman is the glory of the man." This is simply reminding women of their place in creation in the physical sense, for other places in Scripture teach that in our regenerated spirits, both men and women are created in the image of God.

In I Peter 3:6 we find, "Sarah obeyed Abraham,

calling him lord." Notice that "lord" here is not capitalized. When Sarah of Old Testament days called Abraham, "lord," it did not mean he took the place of God in her life, but it meant she was showing her husband honor and respect. "Sir" and "lord" are the same word in both the Greek and Hebrew languages. You can tell only by the context in Scriptures if it is referring to Deity or to man.*Today, we reserve the name Lord for Deity, so it would be more accurate to say Sarah called her husband "Sir."

Some teachers are pressing the example of Sarah, who obeyed her husband Abraham to the extent of lying and saying she was his sister (a half-lie, for she was his half-sister!) and permitting herself to be taken into the harem of the pharaoh. God intervened on her behalf, and therefore, the argument runs, women should obey even a godless husband no matter what he asks them to do. (Abraham, of course, wasn't godless.)

What about Abigail, in I Samuel 25, who specifically disobeyed and deceived her churlish husband and won favor thereby? It is very dangerous to draw an extreme doctrine from one passage in the Scripture.

What of a woman whose husband periodically flies into sadistic rages, and attacks her sexually in such a manner as to cause physical damage? Should she submit to this? What about the husband

---

*The one exception to this is the KJV Bible (and several other translations) which sometimes writes the whole word in capital letters: Lord. That always stands for the personal Name of God.

who demands that his wife submit to an abortion or put their child up for adoption? These are all valid questions in this day and age. Should the Christian wife submit to her husband if he insists that she perform a perverse sexual act? Or take part in a criminal plot? What if he wants her to take drugs? Or to engage in wife-swapping? The answer is obvious, and certainly those who teach an extreme doctrine of submission would not *actually* counsel such things. They are simply idealizing, not thinking the matter through, but such teachings could really lead to harm.

Surely a distinction needs to be made between obeying a husband when he is asking something that is unwise or unfair, but not immoral or unethical, and when he is asking something of his wife that she knows to be against the law of God and man. If it is something she thinks only to be unwise or unfair, then she should share her opinions, if they have a sufficiently open relationship. In the last analysis, she should submit to his decisions and desires, and restrain herself from saying, "I told you so." When he is asking something of his wife that is against the law of God and man, she should not submit, but where possible, lovingly resist his desires, pointing out her reasons.

The wife should, as I see it, obey her husband in every possible way, beyond the call of duty. Often God will change circumstances in a woman's favor as she submits. However, we are accountable for our own sins, and in extreme cases, God must be submitted to above the husband. The Scripture does say to submit to your husband "as unto the Lord" and *not* "as the Lord."

What does God say about worshiping someone other than Himself? The very first commandment God gave to Moses was, "You shall have no other Gods before me. You shall not make for yourself a graven image, or any likeness of anything that is in heaven above, or that is on the earth beneath, or that is in the water under the earth; you shall not bow down to them or serve them; for I the Lord your God am a jealous God" (Deut. 5:7-9a RSV). This commandment takes care of the question nicely. Truly Christian men would never desire to be worshiped; they want only to be respected and loved (Acts 10:25-26).

Headship of the Single Woman

Dear Rita,

More and more, lately, I've been hearing this teaching on "headship." It sounds wonderful for women to be able to depend on their husbands for the major decisions in their lives. However, in my case, I'm divorced and have three little girls. Who provides headship for me? To whom can I turn for Christian help in guiding our lives?

Dear Desiring-Headship,

For all women without husbands—whether they are single, widowed, or divorced—your pastor, the leader of your church family, can give you headship for your major decisions. You should, of course, belong to a church family where the minister has proven himself to be a godly person, whose conduct is in keeping with biblical standards. Speaking to men and women in the Church, Hebrews 13:17 says, "Obey them that have the rule over you, and submit yourselves; for they watch for your souls, as they that must give account, that they may do it with joy, and not with grief: for that is unprofitable for you." Verse seven of that same chapter says further, "Remember them which have the rule over you, who have spoken unto you the word of God: whose faith follow, considering the end of their conversation [conduct]." When there are major decisions in your life, and when after prayer you still don't know what to do, make an appointment with your minister and ask his guidance and help. Your minister is over you in the Lord, and God will often speak through him in a time of need.

A word of warning: This does not mean you're to look on your minister as your "spiritual husband." (If he's married, his wife wouldn't like that idea either.) Anyone who has done frequent counseling knows of the possible danger of emotional attachment with someone of the opposite sex. Don't think this headship means you are to camp on your pastor's doorstep, asking him about all the minor problems and details in your life. Ministers are also busy men, and God has given you common sense to solve small situations.

It is good to have at least three confirmations when making major decisions: one could be from the inner witness of your own regenerated spirit, another from the Scripture, and another through your pastor.* If you're still not sure what to do, fast and pray for the answer you need. Further confirmation may come through attending a Spirit-filled meeting where the Lord may use the gifts of the Spirit, or Bible teaching, or a sermon, to confirm the right direction. You may also want to talk to an additional person—a Bible teacher or counselor who has ministered to you in the past.

In the final analysis, you must be so in tune with the Lord Jesus that you hear from Him yourself. Nevertheless, there is a real safeguard in several confirmations when making decisions.

God has not left you out, my friend in Christ, but He has provided abundantly for all your needs. You are a part of the Body of Christ, and Jesus is the "head of the body, the church" (Col. 1:18). The Church is also called the Bride of Christ, and Jesus is the Bridegroom. Isaiah 54 is literally speaking of the coming glories of Jerusalem, but spiritually, it

---

*For further reading on this subject, see Bob Mumford, *Take Another Look at Guidance* (Plainfield, N.J.: Logos, 1971).

has spoken comfort to numerous women who are without husbands. You can claim verse five for yourself. "For thy Maker [Jesus—the Creator] is thine husband; the Lord of hosts is his name; and thy Redeemer the Holy One of Israel; The God of the whole earth shall he be called." Spiritually speaking, Jesus is your husband. Nothing can surpass being a part of the Bride of Christ and being under His headship.

GROOMING

To see ourselves as others see us.

Looking Dowdy

Dear Rita,

I have a Christian friend who has always in the past dressed in a stylish and attractive manner. Recently I saw her, and she looked absolutely dowdy. She now wears the plainest, most uninteresting clothes, wears no jewelry except her wedding band, and looks like she must not believe in going to a beauty parlor anymore. Is this the way we are to look as Christians? I'm afraid even to phone her, because of her austere look. What do you think has happened, and what will this do to her witness to others?

Dear Afraid-to-Phone,

Following my move to Spokane, Washington in 1964, I found many doors opening for ministry. This led me to live by faith for finances so I could give full time to do the Lord's work. One night I spoke at the home of a Roman Catholic couple. There a young wife, Joan, made sure of her commitment to Jesus that night, and was beautifully baptized with the Holy Spirit. The husband, José, a leading hair stylist, was so impressed by what had happened to his wife that as a gift of gratitude to the Lord he offered to "do" my hair as often as I needed. Thus for nearly two years until I moved to Seattle in 1966, the Lord Jesus not only provided me with a hair dresser but with one that was top-notch. It was obvious that God wanted me to look my best.

When Dennis and I were speaking at a retreat in Scarborough, Yorkshire, in 1968, a college student told me, "You impress me with the attractive way you dress. So many Christians I've known have tried to be holy by looking as unattractive as possible. I wasn't so sure I'd like being a Christian if I was supposed to look like them!"

I believe we women should hit a happy medium. Looking dowdy may be saying, "I don't care enough about others to make the effort to look nice." On the other hand, spending money so extravagantly that we look like clotheshorses won't make a good impression on others or be pleasing to God either.

I had an experience similar to yours. At a Christian retreat, I met an attractive woman who was newly baptized in the Spirit and very happy. Then when I saw her again several years later, I hardly recognized her to be the same person. She now looked pale, unkempt, and awfully plain. Perhaps she was "heavenly minded," but she was very little "earthly good" as a witness.

Often, changes like these take place when people get into groups which teach women that they will become "holy" only as they keep their long list of rules and totally ignore how they look. In sincerely trying to do the right thing, these women end up looking very unappealing.

On the other hand, Christian women can become careless of their appearance because they are so involved with God's work. Something like this happened to me without my realizing it. I used to eat in a particular family-style restaurant in the L.A. area. The owner, a Jewish man, was always so friendly to me and complimented me often on my choice of clothes and so forth. I had witnessed to him by giving him magazines with articles I had written. After I had been away for a few years and returned to visit, some friends and I decided to eat supper in my favorite old restaurant. It didn't seem as if the owner recognized me, so before leaving, I excused myself from my friends and went back to say hello.

He said, "Yes, I recognized you. But what in the world has happened to you? You used to be such an attractive girl!" I just stood there and gulped, made some lame comment, and then said goodbye.

I was truly shocked at his response, and rather hurt. I had not been aware of the change in my appearance. Extremely busy in the work the Lord had given me, I had temporarily forgotten about looking my best as a witness to those who didn't know Him. My close friends no doubt thought I looked fine, but the world evaluates in a different way. My old acquaintance, the restaurant owner, did me a favor to tell it like it was. It was the Lord reminding me that He wanted me to look my best for *Him*.

What would concern me even more than lack of good grooming is the apparent loss of joy in your friend's life. The enemy somehow is robbing her. Don't let him continue to rob her—and you, too—by making you afraid to telephone. You need to let her know that you are thinking about her and would love to have a visit. Your prayers and loving contact may open the doors of fellowship. The Lord then will give you the words to say to help her, I'm sure.

**Humm . . . I guess leaves are out
and skins are in this year.**

Miniskirts vs. Pant Suits

Dear Rita,

What do you think about wearing miniskirts and pant suits? As Christian women, what styles and/or fads are we to go along with? I personally have enjoyed pant suits, feeling they are both feminine and modest, but I can't say the same for miniskirts! What does the Scripture have to say on the subject?

Dear Pro-Pant-Suits,

Woman was created to be a helper, not a hindrance. From the very Genesis of the Bible, we find that a woman can influence man either for good or for evil. Any style that exposes too much of the female figure can be a temptation to a man. Of course, men are responsible to be obedient to God regardless of all wrong influences, yet we Christian women should not add to their temptations. God built into man a normal, healthy attraction to the opposite sex so the human race would continue to reproduce itself; consequently, it doesn't take much to trigger a man's thoughts in this direction.

There aren't any neat little Scripture verses which say, "Thou shalt not wear miniskirts." However, there are a number of verses which speak against improper exposure of the body. The first is when Adam and Eve willfully disobeyed God and then realized they were naked (Gen. 3:7). They were embarrassed and sewed fig leaves together to make "aprons" to clothe themselves. When God came, He reproved them for their sin, and made *coats* out of animal skins for them. Apparently the brief "aprons" were not considered a proper covering. Maybe they were the first miniskirts!

When Moses went up to Mount Sinai to hear from the Lord on behalf of the children of Israel, the people turned from God to idol worship, and outright orgies. Moses was obviously furious when he returned and saw the nakedness of the people and felt they had greatly shamed themselves in front of their enemies (Exod. 32:21-29).

Other Scriptures you may find helpful are Exodus 20:26 (improper exposure at God's altar forbidden), and Exodus 28:40-43 (it was a grave sin for a minister to come into God's presence improperly covered).

In the New Testament, Timothy tells women to "adorn themselves with proper clothing, modestly and discreetly" (I Tim. 2:9 NASB).

I've quoted some Scriptures, and I'm sure you'll find others. The point is not that we must set an ironclad rule that all skirts must come just below the knee, or to the ankles, or to the floor. You know whether an outfit is modest or not. Just ask yourself, "Would I be embarrassed to meet Jesus while wearing this?"

Something must be said about bathing suits. I believe a woman can wear an attractive bathing suit and yet be modest in doing so. A beach coat is a handy garment to wear over your suit—say in walking from the car to the beach. If a woman is attracting too much attention at the beach or pool, then it's time for a new swimsuit. Swimming is wonderful fun and good exercise, so God must have thought it up in the first place. I'm sure He doesn't expect us to wear long red flannels while swimming.

Clothes should be worn to suit the appropriate occasion. A modest bathing suit wouldn't be suggestive at the beach or swimming pool, but downtown shopping, or at a restaurant it would. The time, place, and effect on others should be taken into account when deciding what is right or wrong to wear.

One last point on the subject of nudity. There is nothing evil about the human body; our bodies are "fearfully and wonderfully made." About the first human couple before the Fall, the Scripture says, "They were naked . . . and were not ashamed (Gen. 2:25). It was not intended for the naked human form to be a temptation, but to be a work of art and beauty as well as an instrument to carry out our work in the world. Only after mankind sinned and died spiritually were these gifts of God abused. The basic reason why we must be careful not to expose too much of the body is that we are in a fallen world and also still in the process of being sanctified. In Christian marriage, however the beauty of God's creation may again be enjoyed without shame or embarrassment (Heb. 13:4a).

Now for pant suits. Some Christians are "pro" and others "con" on this subject. Let's take the "cons" first.

The basic Scripture quoted against women wearing long pants or pant suits is found in Deuteronomy 22:5: "A woman shall not wear man's clothing, nor shall a man put on a woman's clothing; for whoever does these things is an abomination to the Lord your God" (NASB). Therefore, for some reason, a woman cannot wear long pants, and a man cannot wear a skirt.

In doing a little research on the subject, I found the word "skirt" in the Bible usually refers to an article of male, not female clothing. Also on Sennacherib's relief (701 B.C.), the elders and important men of the city are shown wearing long dress-like tunics which came down near the ankles. The me-il was a long loose-sleeved robe of public dress. worn mainly by men of official position and by ministers and educators. It could have been like the "coat of many colors" Jacob gave to Joseph or the coat Hannah made for Samuel every year. The basic style must have been used for the high priest's robe, or "robe of the ephod."*

So we can't really say that in Old Testament times men never wore dress-like garments. Although among the Hebrews neither sex was permitted to wear the identical form of clothing used by the other, we see that a few articles of female

*Merrill C. Tenney, ed., The Zondervan Pictorial Bible Dictionary (Grand Rapids, Mich.: Zondervan, 1963), pp. 225-27.

clothing carried somewhat the same basic name and pattern. However, the male and female were *always* distinguishable because of sufficient difference in embroidery, needlework, and other kinds of decoration.*

I bring out these historic facts to clarify some things in our minds. Are priests wrong today for wearing long robed garments at their altars? Was Jesus wrong to wear a long garment? Are the Scotsmen's kilts or knee-length skirts wrong for men to wear in the Highlands or in a parade? Are they breaking the commandment we just quoted from Deuteronomy?

When it comes to women wearing pant suits, the *name* of the garment is not the most important consideration. "If it's a skirt, only women can wear it; if it's long pants, only men can wear them," doesn't follow along with the examples in New Testament times. Rather, we should ask, "Does this article of clothing make me look like a *man* or a *woman*?" It isn't difficult for a woman to select a pant suit that looks both feminine and modest.

A woman in a feminine pant suit isn't trying to look like a man (a lesbian will wear *men's* pants and shirts, not those that are clearly designed for women). The Scotsman who wears kilts is not trying to look like a woman—few things could be more masculine than a kilted Scot in full battle array, knobby knees, and all. This Scripture from Deuteronomy

---

*Ibid., p. 227.

should not be used to prove that certain articles and styles of clothing such as pant suits are evil. To do so is to miss the point God.is making. Look at the Scripture again in the Jerusalem Bible: "A woman must not wear men's clothes nor a man put on women's dress; anyone who does this is detestable to Yahweh your God." God is saying that a man must not put on clothes that are specifically made for a woman, and vice versa, because he or she wants to be, or behave as though they were, of the opposite sex.

This actual exchange of clothing between the sexes, called transvestism, is another thing entirely. It is a symptom of deep self-hatred. It indicates a need for psychological and spiritual healing and restoration, and is a condition of rebellion against God and man which will keep the person from real fellowship with God and man. It is this kind of self-destruction that God is speaking against in Deuteronomy.

Such exchange of garments is related, of course, to actual overt homosexual behavior, and behind that stands Satan, laughing because he has succeeded in degrading and destroying the beautiful things God made. It is not coincidence that sexual confusion, exchange of dress, etc. is a common part of pagan worship.

We as Christian women can work against this confusion of the sexes, not by being legalistic, but by keeping ourselves,* our husbands, and our children looking like the sex God created us and them to be, and loving it. I cannot see how femininely-styled pant suits would add to such confusion. What you do can set the pattern in your home, and influence the world around you.

Wearing a Wig

Dear Rita,

Do you think it's right for a Christian woman to wear a wig, wiglet, or other kind of hairpiece? I'm an outdoors type, loving to swim and play tennis. My husband's work is such that I need to be ready to go out with him to dinner and other social functions at a moment's notice. My hair is rather fine and unmanageable, and a hairpiece would be such a help. What do you think?

Dear Outdoors-Type,

Some women are blessed with strong, thick hair, but others have limp thin hair, and some may

*I am enthusiastic about the old-fashioned long dresses back in style for women today. They are soft and feminine and bring out the womanly charm. It's fun to put on a long frilly dress and go to a prayer meeting, women's fellowship meeting, dinner, church, or a concert.

110

even be bald. Some are able to work with their hair and comb it into lovely styles, and others are in bad shape even the day after going to a beauty parlor. Then there are women like you—always on the go and needing to look your best at all times.

I personally do not feel that there is anything unchristian about wearing a hairpiece. In England, it used to be the custom for men as well as women to wear powdered wigs, and judges in court also wore wigs. John Wesley, a great man of God, wore a wig when he preached in church. It didn't seem to hamper his spirituality or his message.

When a woman knows her hair looks its best, she is much more confident and would naturally be more apt to enjoy meeting new people, a great asset to her husband. If you do decide on a hairpiece, I think it should be as close to your own hair coloring as possible and styled to look like you. In other words, if you're a brunette, I don't think you ought to buy a blonde wig and a red wig and then surprise your husband and his friends by looking like a different person every time they see you!

My situation is similar to yours since my husband and I travel and speak a lot. Although I have currently let my hair grow long, while it was short I especially found wigs and wiglets a great help when I needed to look nice in public on short notice. They were also helpful during that in-between stage while my hair was growing out. Many Christian women use such helps. The idea is to look as natural, as much like you as possible.

I'm doing this for you, dear.

Long Hair

Dear Rita,

I have been letting my hair grow for nearly four years now, but I'm tired of it and in the mood for a change. My husband enjoys my long hair and doesn't want me to have it cut. I'm in a dilemma and need help in making a decision. To cut my hair or not to cut my hair, that is the question.

Dear In-a-Dilemma,

Several years ago, I would have encouraged you to work on your husband until he saw it your way. Now I would say to you that pleasing your husband should be of primary importance.

If your husband disliked long hair and preferred it short, I would say that you should try to please him in this also.

It is amazing how many men, when asked, say that they prefer their wives to wear their hair long. Perhaps God built this desire into their natures. The Scripture teaches that the woman is the glory of the man and the woman's hair is her own glory (I Cor. 11:7,15). "If she wears her hair long, it is a glory to her" (I Cor. 11:15 NGT). In New Testament days, the Hebrews "observed the natural distinction between the sexes by allowing the woman to wear her hair long, while the men restrained theirs by frequent clippings to a moderate length."* (The men's hair was probably just below the ears.)

Perhaps you're bored because you lack ideas and new styles for your hair. Try to find a hairdresser who enjoys working with long hair, or talk to a friend who has long hair and knows how to wear it attractively. If your husband wants your hair long he will most likely be willing to let you purchase the items necessary to keep it well-coiffed.

Recently a friend of mine bought a beautiful thoroughbred dog. His coat was so thick and shiny that I commented on it. She showed me what the breeder told her to purchase to keep his hair that way: wheat germ oil, vitamins and minerals; cottage cheese was to be mixed with his meat each day, and I don't know what all. It's surprising how people will make the effort to feed their animals so well and yet often forget that if those things are so good for pets, how good they would also be for human beings. In order to have beautiful hair, watch your diet.

Protein shampoos and conditioners are good for your hair. Sometimes I beat a raw egg into my shampoo to give my hair a treat. Have fun with long hair and see just how luxurious you can help it become. Take good care of your "glory."

---

*McClintock and Strong, Op. cit., vol. IV, p. 24.

Eye Makeup

Dear Rita,

Do you think it is okay for a Christian woman to wear mascara and other eye makeup? I think that the emphasis being put on the eyes these days is very attractive, yet recently a minister likened it to following Jezebel's example. I certainly don't want to be like her, but at the same time am not sure about the validity of this teaching either.

Dear Not-Sure,

Long dark eyelashes are a becoming feature. Some people are endowed with them naturally, and others are not so fortunate. If darkening the lashes enhances the beauty of the eyes God created, I can't see any difference between that and wearing attractive clothes or having your hair styled.

Lining the eyes or applying mascara should be done with discretion so that it is not obvious. Vonda Kay Van Dyke, former Mis America and a devout Christian, said in her book, *Dear Vonda Kay*, that some ladies complimented her, "because it was refreshing to see a girl in her position who didn't wear eye liner and all that sort of stuff." She thanked them and said, "I do wear it, and the fact that you didn't realize it is a nice compliment."*

*Vonda Kay Van Dyke, *Dear Vonda Kay* (Westwood, New Jersey: Revell, 1967), p. 20. A book for teenagers.

Now back to Jezebel. You're right—she's no one to pattern your life after! Yet her sin was not that she "painted her face" (II Kings 9:30),* but that her whole life was wicked. She did not worship the true God of Abraham, Isaac, and Jacob, but rather had from childhood been a strong worshiper of the Ba'alim. The worship of many of these idols undoubtedly involved forms of ritual prostitution in which Jezebel very likely took part. She also practiced witchcraft. Continuously, Jezebel worked to convert the people of Israel to her faith, and she killed all the prophets of Jehovah she could lay hands on.

God was especially angry when she connived to have a good man, Naboth, killed by stoning—after a mock trial—so that her husband, King Ahab, could get his property. Naboth had previously refused to sell the land because it was his family's inheritance.

The prophet Elijah foretold a horrible death for Jezebel, which was fulfilled some years later, when Jehu exercised vengeance on the whole family of Ahab. It is at this time that Jezebel "painted her eyelids and fixed her hair" (II Kings 9:30 TLB)* before she looked out of the window to taunt Jehu for her husband's death.

---

*In Hebrew, it literally says she "put her eyes in paint"; therefore, this cannot be taken as a Scripture against rouge and lipstick as some have used it. McClintock and Strong, *Op. cit.*, vol. III, pp. 427-428.

*"Painting the eyes," or rather the eyelids, scarcely appears in the Authorized Version, as the translators, unaware of the custom, usually render "eye" by "face," although "eye" is still preserved in the margin. McClintock and Strong, *Op. cit.*, vol. III, p. 427.

In ancient Egypt and Assyria, the practice of painting the eyes was common. They blackened the edge of the eyelids, both above and below the eyes, with a black powder called *kohl*. This practice was not as frequent among the Hebrews, however, It is interesting to note, though, that one of Job's daughters from the family God restored to him was called *Kerenhappukh* meaning "horn of eye-paint" (Job 42:14).**

It is true that in three other places in the Old Testament where painting the eyes is mentioned, it is connected with prostitution (Jer. 4:30; Ezek. 23:40; Prov. 6:25). However, Jezebel was probably not trying to lure Jehu, but rather it was a matter of defiant vanity, as she always painted her eyes before she showed herself publicly.

Jehu called on some of the servants who were standing by Jezebel to throw her from the window. When, a little later, Jehu gave the order for the burial of her body, they could find only her skull, her feet, and the palms of her hands—the dogs had eaten all the rest, as Elijah had prophesied (II Kings 9:30-37). Her tragic end was not because she wore eye makeup, as some have taught or intimated, but rather to show the end of those who deal unjustly with God's people, follow after false gods, and engage in other evil practices.

We are living in New Testament days, and using

**"The eye paint was kept in a small horn or ornamental metal vase with a thin rod for applying it." James Hastings, ed. *A Dictionary of the Bible* (New York: Charles Scribner's Sons, 1911), vol. I, p. 814.

eye makeup does not necessarily mean a woman's heart is set to do evil! The time and the custom of the day is an important consideration. Not too many years ago, when a woman wore lipstick, it meant she was "on the loose." This obviously not the case today.

In the past few years, no lipstick or very pale lipstick has actually been the style. It's interesting that while the use of lipstick has been frowned upon by several denominations, those same churches don't have much to say against eye makeup. Many of their women use some eye makeup, wear little or no lipstick, groom their hair nicely, and look right in style today.

The styles weren't so easy for me when I was in high school. Although I learned many good things in the church of my youth, their stand against wearing makeup of any kind was not helpful. In the ninth grade, all the other girls were wearing lipstick. I wanted to wear it too. Looking so pale in contrast to the other girls, I would put it on when I got to school and wipe it off before I got home.

I found from this experience that teaching against makeup does nothing but condemn a person and ends up helping to draw them away from Jesus. If I couldn't keep the rule of no-lipstick, and the many others added to it, I reasoned to myself, then there was no sense in trying to live a Christian life. Thus began a wilderness journey which ended in 1960 when I was set free in God's Spirit.*

*For Rita's story, see "Second Chance," *Aglow Magazine*, Issue #11, Fall 1972, pp. 4-11.

Now that I realize that God loves me whether or not I wear lipstick, eye makeup, and fingernail polish, I wear very little of any of them—not because it's wrong, but for entirely different reasons. Mascara always seems to smudge and makes me look as if I have dark circles under my eyes! Also, since I became a charismatic Christian, something funny often happens to me when I am blessed by the Lord —tears begin to flow. When I have on mascara, I tend to hold back these tears of joy, and miss out on the full release God has for me. Nothing is worth missing out on God's blessing!

In these last thirteen years of praying for numerous women, I have seen many tears mingled with eye makeup. If all of them were put together, what a black stream there would be! Some companies advertise waterproof mascara, but I have yet to see it proven. Anyway, I'm glad that mascara is not God-proof, and that He loves all women regardless of whether they use eye makeup or not.

The Lord Jesus again and again points out that the exterior is not the most important thing to Him but rather the motive of our heart within. If a woman makes up her eyes to be seductive, the Lord knows that; and if she does it to look more attractive as a witness for Him, the Lord knows that, too.

What *all* of us as women will find most becoming is to "anoint our eyes with eyesalve," as this is what Jesus counseled the Church to do (Rev. 3: 18b). In the natural sense, "eyesalve was a preparation used for healing or strengthening the eye."* Spiritually, it speaks of healing and restoring our spiritual vision, which was marred by sin. No matter what we put on or don't put on our eyelids and eyelashes, may our eyes be open to the vision and understanding God wants us to have today, and may our eyes reflect the beauty of Jesus.

---

*James Hastings, Op. cit., vol. I, p. 814.

PROBLEMS

Bloom where you're planted.

Unspiritual Husband

Dear Rita,

I've been married several years, and a year ago met Jesus and soon after was baptized with the Holy Spirit. My husband is not a believer and therefore not interested in spiritual things; we have nothing in common in this area. I want to grow in the Spirit, but he does nothing but hold me back; he doesn't even want me to go to church on Sundays. I've recently come to the conclusion that if I am going to grow spiritually, it will have to be without him.

Dear Held-Back,

Remember your husband was your choice. There must have been many things about him which were wonderful. You might want to write those things down to refresh your memory. It isn't necessary for you to have a Christian husband in order to grow spiritually. In fact, some people grow faster in the Lord when they have trials, because it is then necessary to rely on Jesus more constantly.

Other Christian women have had similar situations. Look at I Peter 3:1-3a, 4: "Likewise wives, being subject* to your own husbands, that, even if any are disobedient to the Word [this could include non-

---

*A major Greek Lexicon defines "subject" as "voluntary yielding in love." It comes from *hypotage,* meaning "obedience," and is the same word as is used in Ephesians 5:21 and I Peter 5:5. Arndt and Gingrich, *Op. cit.* p. 855.

believers] they may be gained [or won] having witnessed your chaste conduct carried out in fear [meaning awe or healthy respect for God]." The apostle Peter goes on to say that wives should not be overly concerned with adorning the exterior person but "the hidden man [your spirit, the new creature] of the heart, in the incorruptible [ornament] of the meek [humble and teachable] and quiet spirit, which is before God of great price."*

These Scriptures certainly teach that a woman can grow in the Spirit even though a husband is not obeying God or not even born of the Spirit himself. In fact, her growth in that incorruptible life God has given her will so transform her conduct that the husband may be won to God. You are one-hundred percent correct to desire spiritual progress, but this will occur to the fullest only as you come God's way and according to God's pattern.

I have a friend in another city whose husband suddenly began to be infuriated every time she went to church on Sunday. She prayed about this and felt the Lord was instructing her to stop going to church on Sunday but to go instead to one or two weekly prayer and Bible study groups during the day, when her husband was at work.* Her husband was abso-

---

*George Ricker Berry. The Interlinear Greek-English New Testament (Grand Rapids, Mich.: Zondervan, 1958). The word "ornament" is implied and is in brackets as it appears in the original. All brackets here are mine.

*Any woman who feels this might be a good direction to take must be getting fellowship somewhere during this time. Also, if there are children, she must see that they get to a good Sunday school, and young people's fellowship.

lutely floored the first few Sundays she stayed home with him. My friend, realizing that she was under the headship and authority of her husband, felt that by her submission to him, God would be able to deal with him directly. After she had stayed away from church several months, her husband began to actually encourage her to return. I don't know what else has happened, but one thing is sure—their house is not a turmoil on Sundays as it used to be, and her husband is not being continuously established in a weekly habit of getting steaming mad at God.

The KJV translation of I Peter 3:1 speaks of the man being won by the "conversation" of the wife. Today when we hear the word "conversation" we think of "informal talking," but the Bible word doesn't mean this at all; instead, it means "behavior" or, as the Interlinear says, "conduct." I bring this out in case you might feel it is saying that you must win your husband through verbal witness. Some women even try to make a second-handed witness to their husbands when talking to friends on the telephone while he is within hearing distance! (By the way, watch those long telephone calls when your hubby is home—show him respect in this way.) Verbal witnessing to the people closest to you is the hardest thing to do effectively, and when tried, often causes a reaction opposite to the one hoped for.

Recently, I saw a motto on a pretty banner decorated with orange and yellow flowers which very nicely capped what I am trying to say: "Bloom where you are planted." "Held-back," hold on! You are about to grow like anything, and before long, I believe your husband will be growing right along with you.

Substitute Husband

Dear Rita,

The pastor of our church is a wonderful man, baptized with the Spirit, who gives unselfishly of his time. I don't know where I'd be if he hadn't helped me over some very rough times spiritually and helped me with my marriage also. Even though my husband is a Christian, he's not living it much of the time, and I don't feel nearly as free talking to him as I do to my pastor. We have real *rapport* together, and I have also been used by the Holy Spirit to minister to his needs many times. My neighbor tells me I am wrong, and that I'm using my pastor as a sort of substitute husband. She says that I'm being unfair to my husband, my pastor, and also my pastor's wife. I feel that as long as my pastor can help me better than my husband can, I should continue to go to him. Do you agree?

Dear Endangered,

You may be walking into or unknowingly creating an enticing trap. It is doubtful whether any man and woman who are continually associated together, especially if they are sharing about personal things, can maintain what is sometimes called a platonic relationship. We hear now and then of a minister who has left his family in favor of his secretary, or his choir directress, and many think it strange that a man of God would take such a tumble, yet the basic reason is simple—they were together in close quarters too often. Too many Christian homes have been broken up by seemingly innocent beginnings. The opportunity for the enemy to work in this way must be avoided at all costs. The Bible clearly tells us to avoid the very appearance of evil. (I Thess. 5:22).

If you need to talk with your minister confidentially, you can do so at his office, with his secretary in the vicinity. "Behind closed doors" sessions can be an open invitation to problems. If you need to consult with him frequently, it might be wiser to ask if you can talk with him at his house, with his wife invited to be present. Ask yourself, "Do I really want his advice if I have to have his wife present to get it?" Any long continued counseling situation between a man and woman is not wise. You may think you and/or your pastor are completely above such matters, but do not be deceived. The flesh is weak.

It is no more advisable for you to be ministering to your pastor in private than it is ever for men and women to be ministering to one another in private, unless of course their relationship is such that there should be no problem—i.e., they are married, or engaged, or family members. Even in a group situation, it is not good for you to have some kind of special relationship to your pastor that is obvious to the others. Spiritual attachment moves over so quickly to psychological and physical attachment. Gifts of the Holy Spirit must not be used in such a way as to make another person's husband dependent on you.

Even if you are sure your motives are pure, avoid further complications. Have you ever thought of talking to a reliable Christian woman with some knowledge of counseling? This would be much safer. If your problems are very serious, it might be wise to see a qualified Christian psychologist or psychiatrist.

It would be a surprise to me if your husband was not feeling the competition of your pastor's place in your life. This may drive him further away from you and from the Lord. I once heard it put this way: "Your husband will not cherish you if you are letting any other man do the cherishing." If you find after breaking up this close fellowship that you miss it more than you should, it might be best for you and your husband to ask the Lord to guide you to another church home.

Many good people have been warned in time, and awakened before they went too far—to the point of no return—in a wrong relationship. You can thank your neighbor for being honest enough to warn you. Others may have felt the same way, but lacked the courage to talk to you about it. May God bless and guide you and keep you in the center of His love and will.

When you're mad, count to nine . . .

Quick Temper

Dear Rita,

I have had a quick temper most of my life. In the past, it has always been excused on the grounds that I have red hair. As a Christian, I realize that the color of my hair can no longer be blamed for my temper. Having been undisciplined in this area most of my life, what can I do now to help myself, my husband, and family?

Dear Redhead,

You know the advice we've been given through the years: If you're mad at someone, count to ten before you say anything? I heard something far better recently: If you are really mad, count to nine by naming the nine fruits of the Holy Spirit.

A short time after I heard this, something happened to get me stirred up, so I thought, "I'll just count to nine." I started counting with the first fruit, love, and that's as far as I needed to count. With the remembrance of the forgiving love of God toward me and everyone else, I couldn't hold a grudge.

Memorize the fruit of the Spirit so you, too, can count to nine: love, joy, peace, patience, kindness, goodness, faithfulness, humility, discipline (Gal. 5:22-23 au. para.). It's interesting that the ninth fruit is discipline (self-control), what you particularly expressed a need for.

I'm glad to hear that the old wives' tale about the results of having red hair has been exposed by the Holy Spirit. The enemy of our souls enjoys giving reasons for our sins so that we will excuse them, keeping them as seemingly harmless pets rather than getting rid of them. Having a bad temper is like harboring a wild beast in your backyard. You can either keep feeding him three square meals a day, or you can give him the bare daily rations, or you can stop feeding him altogether. This third choice is, I'm sure, what you have in mind.

Jesus Christ possibly had red or auburn hair; at least that's how Flavius Josephus, a Jewish historian living in the first century, described Him. Can you imagine Jesus using the excuse of red hair for a temper? There is only one place in the New Testament where I find the statement that Jesus was angry. This was when the Pharisees were watching Him closely to see if He would break the law by healing on the Sabbath so they would have something on Him. Before healing the man, Jesus asked, "Is it lawful to do good on the sabbath days, or to do evil?" (Mark 3:4). But they wouldn't answer Him. He then looked at them "with anger, being grieved for the hardness of their hearts (Mark 3:5a). Jesus looked into their hearts and was angered at the work of His ancient enemy, Satan, active within these men.

Another place where it looks as if Jesus was angry (although the word isn't used) was when He found the priests and scribes selling sacrificial animals in the Temple at a great financial profit. He cleansed the Temple by overthrowing their tables and chasing the men out (Matt. 21:12-15). This was the only kind of anger Jesus had, anger with the enemy and his co-workers.

On the other hand, one can think of numerous places in the Scriptures where Jesus was unjustly treated, and yet responded with gentleness and love. Even when He was being nailed to the Cross unjustly, Jesus was praying for God His Father to forgive those who were crucifying Him. Jesus was not an "angry young man" as some today have tried to portray Him.

Jesus also taught that the things we put into our mouths do not defile our souls but what comes out of our mouths will (Matt. 15:17-18). Bad temper and angry words will defile us. We can pray as the psalmist David: "Set a watch, O Lord, before my mouth; keep the door of my lips."

The Book of Ephesians gives us these instructions: "If you're angry, do not sin: don't let the sun go down upon your wrath: neither give any place to the devil." Apparently it is possible to be angry without sinning, but we must not allow the devil to turn it into hatred or to use it for his purposes, nor must we hold on to it and let it smoulder in our hearts. This is a verse my husband and I have put into practice from the first of our marriage. If one of us has said or done something hurtful (most often unknowingly), neither of us can go to sleep until we've talked it out, asked forgiveness, and have prayed about it—even if it's one o'clock in the morning. This way the enemy cannot get a wedge in between husband and wife which he would then try to enlarge. I highly recommend the application of this verse to your life.

The Epistle of James admonishes us further: "Let every man be quick to hear, slow to speak, slow to anger, for the anger of man does not work the righteousness of God" (James 1:19 RSV). That's good advice, isn't it? "Quick to hear" and "slow to speak."

Next time you need help and after you've counted to nine, you might try praying "in the Spirit" (I Cor. 14:14-15). for a little while. That should slow you down a bit. After calling upon God, when you do speak, I believe your words will be full of love and joy.

Honestly facing your need and sincerely wanting to change are two of the first steps in receiving God's help. Since you've already taken these steps, the rest will surely follow.

Kick the Smoking Habit

Dear Rita,

I recently received the Baptism in the Holy Spirit but still can't seem to quit smoking! My husband had no problem giving it up; I guess he's stronger, or more obedient than I am. What can I do to accomplish surrender in this area of my life?

Dear Smoker,
There are many reasons why people begin the smoking habit. Psychology tells us that often the habit can be traced back to the infant's unsatisfied need to be held and loved by his mother. In this case, a cigarette is like a pacifier, offering oral satisfaction. Picturing a woman with a baby bottle or pacifier in her mouth certainly isn't appealing, but in fact, that may be what it means to her sub-consciously. Prayer for healing of the emotions and help from a Christian counsellor may be needed.

Others got started with this habit because as youngsters they were told that smoking was evil, and being rebellious, just naturally wanted to try it. It also was a way to hit back at parents and assert one's independence.

Some people smoke because they think it is the sophisticated thing to do, and they want to be accepted by friends they admire who smoke. There is also a kind of fellowship in it: "You light my cigarette and I'll light your cigarette." (Advertising has done much to get this idea across.)

Insecure people may feel more superior to others and on top of things when they are smoking. They may feel awkward or self-conscious and, not knowing what else to do with their hands, just keep smoking.

People also smoke because they don't have the willpower to curb their eating habits, and take up smoking as a substitute; the taste buds are dulled so that food doesn't have the appeal it used to.

Many people are just plain bored.* A general statement for all these categories could be that people smoke because they have a deep unmet need in their lives. That inner need is often met when a person meets Jesus Christ as Savior and/or receives the Baptism with the Holy Spirit; the need being met, smoking naturally ceases.

As for your battle in trying to give up smoking, I know what you're talking about, although I was a serious smoker for only five years or so. Looking back on it now, I realize one of the reasons I smoked was in rebellion against my religious background. I wanted to be "with it" and accepted by my peer group. Also, I was curious to know why so many people liked to smoke.

One day, as I was coming back to the Lord and beginning to re-experience the relationship I had with Him in my childhood, I realized while praying in church that I was thinking about my next cigarette, rather than thinking about God. Was I going to put God in second place to this habit the rest of my life? A short time later, just before I was renewed in the power of the Holy Spirit, I turned my life back over to Jesus. With this I prayed, "Dear Father, if You want me to give up smoking, please

---

*Eileen Guder, *God, But I'm Bored!* (New York, N. Y.: Dell Publishing Co., 1972).

take the desire for cigarettes away from me." Then I added, "If You do this, Lord, I will never smoke again." The empowering of the Holy Spirit, immediately following this prayer, met the inner needs of which smoking was an outward symptom, and from the fall of 1960 until now, I haven't smoked again. I now think too much of myself (Jesus taught me to love myself) to take years off my life by filling my lungs with tar.

I have often thought that there is a destructive spirit from the enemy which helps to keep a person smoking even when he or she wants to stop. I remember smoking a number of times even when I had tonsillitis and a raw throat, or a bad cold. I have a lovely friend who has emphysema and yet continues to make her condition worse by smoking. Another friend who was in social work had to have a lung removed, but continued to smoke, even at times when she was having trouble breathing. She died at an early age. It reminds me of the Scripture describing Satan saying, "The thief comes not, but for to steal, kill and to destroy" (John 10:10a). Continuous smoking can take years off a person's life, as the medical warnings these days bear proof. Yet some people must think very little of themselves, because they keep right on smoking.

Some Christians, because they do not find chapter and verse in the Bible against smoking, think that's an excuse to smoke. They want to find an additional commandment which says, "Thou shalt not smoke." But the whole Bible speaks of the fact that

God would come to dwell in people, and that His people, those who have received Christ, would become temples of the Holy Spirit. "What? Do you not know that your body is the temple of the Holy Ghost which is in you, which you have of God, and you are not your own? For you are bought with a price: therefore glorify God in your body" (I Cor. 6:19-20).

A young man with a bad smoking habit and a background of condemnation about it was seated on an airplane next to a well-known singer and evangelist. After visiting a bit, the young man said, "Say, Tony, can I smoke cigarettes and still go to heaven?" Tony thought a moment and replied, "Yes!" Then he added with a smile, "You'll get there a whole lot faster, too."

Judging people on the basis of an external habit may be the means of keeping them away from meeting Jesus. My husband, Dennis, and I boarded a flight from Chicago to Minneapolis several years ago. When flying commercially, we generally pray and ask God to give us a person to witness to. As we walked down the aisle, we felt led to sit next to a blind man, probably in his early fifties. He was tall with a pleasant look on his face, toying absentmindedly with his white cane. Dennis took the seat next to him and I sat next to the aisle.

In a short time, Dennis and his neighbor were in conversation. The man was from a Pentecostal background, and not only that, his father was a minister. When Dennis asked if he was a Christian, the man replied, "Oh, no, I've never been able to give up cigarettes." We were both amazed by his statement, realizing that his concept of what it meant to be a Christian was actually keeping his soul from eternal life. My husband talked with him further, and finally led him in a prayer to receive Jesus as his Savior, while I sat there praying quietly and rejoicing within. When our new Christian brother was leaving the airplane, he told us that the tape recorder he was carrying had a tape of the Gospel of John on it which he had just received that week but hadn't listened to yet. The Lord had surely set the stage for our visit with him, and as he listened to the Scriptures, I'm sure they came alive for him. As far as his smoking is concerned, a friend of ours says, "God catches His fish before He cleans them." I'm sure God helped him with his smoking habit and no doubt with other more serious problems.

To list some of the things I believe may help you and others kick the smoking habit:

1. Meet Jesus as Savior.
2. Be baptized in the Holy Spirit.
3. Consecrate your life to Jesus; present your body to Him.
4. Evaluate your reasons for smoking, and pray for healing of your emotions and memories.
5. Receive prayer for deliverance.
6. Forgive everyone, and know that God has forgiven you.
7. Check on your dietary habits.

8. Limit contacts with old smoking buddies (at least until you're stronger); choose new friends who don't smoke.
9. Figure out how much money is wasted on cigarettes each year, including clothes you've burnt holes in, and plan something worthwhile to do with it.
10. Figure out how much time you spend on buying and smoking cigarettes each year.
11. Make it a point to see a movie showing the effects of smoking on the lungs.
12. Start a program of physical exercise; teach yourself discipline in this way.
13. Spend fifteen minutes or more each morning in prayer and Bible study.

This answer to your letter turned out to be an epistle, yet I'm sure there are still other aspects not mentioned here. While you're working on this problem in your life, remember, God loves you right now—just as you are. Don't let frustration or condemnation come into your life; they will just send you in the wrong direction. At the same time, remember that God has a wonderful plan for your life which you can thwart by throwing away years of priceless life in this harmful pastime.

Concentrate on God's great love for you, and then just love Him with all your being. Soon you'll be a happy non-smoker—I'm sure!

Jesus to the rescue!

Resist Temptation

Dear Rita,

Please don't quote my name if you use this question, because I wouldn't want anyone to know about my situation. For the past year, I have been in love with my pastor. Even though he's married to a nice wife and has several children and though he has never said so, I know he feels the same way about me. On Sundays I hardly hear the sermon, because all I can think of is this man. I try to put these thoughts out of my mind, but in a few minutes, they are back stronger than ever. I take part in every church activity so I can be where he is, even though I know I shouldn't. Should I go to him and tell him how I feel and ask his advice? Please help me, but don't ask me to change churches. My family has been part of this church for three generations, and I could never explain if I wanted to quit going there.

Dear In-Love-with-Pastor,

What does it mean to be in love? As I see it, love is caring about another person more than you do yourself or anyone else in this world. It's not wanting to hurt that person in any way. It's helping that person to be fulfilled in every area: spirit, soul, and body. It's desiring their love for God to grow beyond all loves. True love would not do anything to come between a person and God. It's wanting God's first best for that person's life and working to that end. When a Christian has found the right person to spend his or her earthly life with, God will confirm this to his or her spirit, and it will be in agreement with the Scripture.

It is obvious that loving and desiring a married man and pursuing him is against everything that truly is love. Let's face it—the direction you are going could ultimately lead to breaking apart a family!

You've asked for help, so here goes. First of all, you must determine in your own heart that the way you've been headed is wrong. Next is to stop taking part in church activities where your pastor will be present. You may feel you have to continue to attend church on Sunday mornings but try to find another church or women's Bible study or prayer group where you can be spiritually fed during the week. For a year, the enemy has stolen your spiritual food by making your ears deaf to what God wanted to say to you, and therefore you are more of an easy prey. James 1:14-15 says: "But every man is tempted when he is drawn away of his own lust, and enticed Then when lust hath conceived, it brings forth sin: and sin, when it is finished, brings forth death."

If you do what you know is right, I don't think you will need to talk things over with your pastor. If he is personally drawn to you, talking to him might increase the temptation in his own life and lead to trouble. If it is all on your part, it would be a great source of embarrassment to you both and to you in particular. The Lord has the right man for you to marry; but you are making it impossible for this to come to pass by living in a fantasy world.

Pastors have to realize that unhappily married or single women who admire them, especially those to whom they have ministered in counseling and prayer, can mistake the love of God for human love. This may happen even in situations where there has been very little contact.

If after taking the steps I have recommended, you are still having serious trouble controlling your thought life, prayer for healing and deliverance in this area may be helpful. Go to a reputable pastor or counselor who is active in the charismatic renewal for help along these lines.

Your future depends on what you put into your life today. Just as the farmer has a choice about the seeds he sows into the ground, so we have a choice about the seed thoughts we put into our lives. One of the greatest powers we have is to choose what we will think about. We act upon what we think, and we will eventually reap what we sow in the field of our minds.

For me, one of the most helpful Scriptures on a victorious thought life has been: "Casting down imaginations, and every high thing that exalts itself against the knowledge of God, and bringing into captivity every thought to the obedience of Christ" (II Cor. 10:5). With this Scripture, I sometimes picture Jesus as a cowboy on His horse. When an unworthy thought tries to lodge in my mind, I yell for Jesus. He comes galloping up on His speedy stallion, and encircles that thought with His lasso, removing it from me instantly. Jesus takes that thought captive, and I'm set free.

The mind is a real battleground. Your mind has been bombarded by wrong thoughts for a year, which though you resisted, you also at the same time tempted yourself, and so the thoughts have remained. When territory has been yielded to the enemy, he doesn't give it up without a fight. It is going to take some effort on your part; but Jesus is on your side, others will stand with you, and that ground will be regained. Jesus, on His white stallion, is right around the corner; give a call for help and He'll be right there!

Condemnation

Dear Rita,

At a recent Holy Spirit mission, I thought I received the Baptism in the Holy Spirit, but since returning home have felt guilty, condemned, and actually unredeemed. I need help!

I will give you some background. I awoke at the age of seven, at a revival meeting, in time to hear about the unpardonable sin and to hear the preacher say, "If you don't want to go to hell, step forward." I stepped forward. I don't remember praying to receive Jesus Christ at all. I was a sinful little kid and grew up to be a sinful big kid.

I was married in my teenage years and began having children during the time my husband was working and going to the university. All this added pressure to my life, and several years after our marriage, I awoke one night "feeling" lost, condemned, as if I had committed the unpardonable sin. After several weeks of torment, my pastor and I were praying at the church and the burden lifted. I "felt" the glory of the Lord for a couple of days, I thought, and claimed this as my saving experience and was baptized in a nearby river.

I fell away, however, became involved in some flagrant sinning, and everything began to fall apart. Unhappy, I erroneously thought the Lord had let me down and began a heathen life for a number of years. My sins were gross, involving addiction to alcohol, and adultery that followed drunkenness. My husband forgave me after I confessed all to him. In 1969 at a revival meeting, I made a hand-raising re-commitment to the Lord and then tried honestly to turn away from sin. A year later, following a party where I had one too many, I asked the Lord to come into my life, based on Revelation 3:20. I believed I had made peace with the Lord, but didn't tell anyone about this except with a changed life which I really tried to change. Lately I have been having doubts and losing interest in witnessing, although I believe I have led several people to the Lord.

At any rate, I received instruction and believed that I received the Baptism with the Holy Spirit, and was on "Cloud Nine." I felt I was a Christian while receiving instruction. A week later, I became burdened but didn't know why. Then, BOOM! I was filled with depression, guilt, condemnation, confusion, and a feeling of lostness.

I'm in a mess. Could you shed some light on my problem? I have been telling myself to trust Him regardless of how I feel, but I should be Spirit-filled and happy instead of depressed and feeling condemned. I have once again thought that I must have committed the unpardonable sin. Can you help me? Please?

Dear In-Need,

From what I can see from your letter, the teaching from your youth has heaped guilt and condemnation on your head from the very beginning. This kind of background has the tendency to cause people to rebel, because the rules are so rigid that it's nearly impossible for anyone to keep them. The erroneous idea sort of goes this way: Every time you sin, God leaves you. But the Scripture says about Jesus: "For He has said, I will never, never leave you, and I will not, I will not, I will not forsake you" (Heb. 13:5b free translation from NGT). This is the way it reads in the literal Greek text. Once we've invited Jesus in, He does *not* leave us. We may feel that He has left us, because sin separates us from the sense of God's presence, but when we put things right, that relationship is re-established immediately. Jesus hasn't left us—*we* have left Him!

Here is an ingrained pattern: A person sins in a small way, and because he thinks God has left him, communication is broken. Since God has "let him down," all seems to be lost, and he thinks he might as well go further into sin. In this way, a life gets more and more messed up, and the enemy has a "heyday" messing up a temple of the Holy Spirit. Then this person hears an evangelist, gets re-convicted, and dedicates his life again, but still without receiving the power of the Holy Spirit. Later, he may go through the same painful process all over again.

Some ministers with only the basic teachings of sin, salvation, and hell, keep the people coming to church through fear. Hebrews 6:1 says, "Therefore leaving the principles of the doctrine of Christ [not giving them up, but now that we know them, let's build upon them] *let us go on.*" If Christians aren't moving on with Christ, they may fall back and lose much of the progress they have made.

You have *not* committed the unpardonable sin. If you had, you would have no interest in or desire for Jesus—your heart would be totally hardened against God. That obviously isn't your case. My husband and I believe that this Scripture (Matt. 12:32) doesn't refer to believers at all, but speaks of those who constantly harden their hearts against God each time the Holy Spirit deals with them, until at some point they become totally disinterested. If a person could look at the things Jesus did and attribute them to the devil, and continue to do so throughout his lifetime, that person could never become a true believer in Jesus Christ, could he? Therefore, this sin is unpardonable because the person has no desire to ask for pardon—not believing in God anyway. In other words, the sin is unforgivable because forgiveness is never asked for nor received.

You may have picked up this irrational fear of committing the unpardonable sin from some of the sermons you heard in your youth. The enemy draws upon them to bring you under condemnation. Remember, it is Satan who condemns, but the Holy Spirit *convicts* for *definite* sins. The Holy Spirit is specific, and doesn't leave us with a vague feeling of conviction for we know not what. A wonderful Scripture for your meditation is, "There is therefore now no condemnation to them which are in Christ Jesus, who walk not after the flesh, but after the Spirit" (Rom. 8:1).

If you remember any erroneous, fear-producing statements in regard to these feelings of condemnation, spoken by anyone—even ministers or parents—realize that these things have no power over you, and by an act of your will, refuse all feeling of condemnation in Jesus' Name. As you have confessed your sins to Jesus, He has certainly forgiven you, and He loves you.

Have you seen a copy of our book, *The Holy Spirit and You?* I believe it would be helpful to you. The chapter on discerning of spirits has a section telling about casting away the influence of the enemy. These wrong influences are like fiery darts, which can be resisted in Jesus' Name. You can make a prayer something like this for each evil work of the enemy: "Spirit of condemnation, I bind you in the Name of Jesus, and under His precious Blood; I cast you away from me in Jesus' Name!" Here's a suggested list to pray about in this way: spirit of condemnation, spirit of unbelief, lying spirit, tormenting spirit, spirit of depression, spirit of guilt, deceiving spirit, spirit of confusion, and anything else the Holy Spirit shows you as you pray. You may want to pray alone or with someone about these things. After such prayer, get your eyes on Jesus and keep them there. The Bible says to be "simple concerning evil" (Rom. 16:19b), so don't spend much time in this activity. Know that you have authority over the enemy. Resist him and he must flee.

I would also recommend that you get a copy of the book, *Release of the Spirit*, by Watchman Nee. You *must* understand the difference between your soul *(psyche)* and spirit *(pneuma)* in order to understand what has happened to you in the past and to know how to cope with your present situation. When you were feeling on "Cloud Nine" after the Baptism in the Spirit, all was well with you and God; that was your regenerated spirit gaining strength over your old life patterns. Then, when you doubted God and felt condemned, that was your soul getting back on top, controlling things with the assistance of the enemy, Satan. Feelings or emotions are in the soul realm and cannot be relied upon. We must grow and develop in our spirits so we are not influenced in the soulish, vacillating part of our beings. As we walk in the Spirit, our souls are restored and stabilized.

People with Christian backgrounds who knowingly walk away from God and establish bad habit patterns over a period of time will naturally have greater battles for a while after they return to the Lord, and the battle will especially be in the area of the mind (part of the soul). You need to learn how to immediately cast out every thought that contradicts God's Word, and to get your mind back on that which is good and true. The more you do this, having frequent fellowship with other charismatic believers, and praying in the Holy Spirit language God has given you, the less difficult the battle will be, and you will walk in a greater awareness of the Holy Spirit.

Get a concordance and go through the Bible, writing down every Scripture that confirms your salvation, and that shows God has removed your sins (e.g., Ps. 103:10-17; Isa. 1:18; I John 1:7,9; 5:11-15). You might copy such Scriptures for easy reference, and read them each day before you pray. Listen to good tapes with positive messages, and go to church where the minister speaks life, not condemnation. Let God heal your memories.

You have invited Jesus to come into your life; you have confessed your sins and have no doubt put things right where possible; you have asked for and received the Baptism with the Holy Spirit. If you will do the other things mentioned in this letter, as the Holy Spirit guides, you are bound to have victory. God has begun a wonderful work in your life, and He always completes what He begins.

On the back of a sand and gravel truck, I once saw a sign which read, "Find a need and fill it." The thought came to me that that's exactly what God does. He will fill your every need with the power of His presence and His love. Then you can be like the fellow in the truck (your truck will be full of God's healing love, instead of sand and gravel); after having your own needs met, you'll be able to fill up the emptiness in other people's lives. That's when things will really get exciting. And that's exactly what God has in store for you!

SPIRITUAL
LIFE

"Ye shall be My witnesses,"
(more effective ones if ye are prepared) . . .

Preparing to Witness

Dear Rita,

Recently while visiting an old friend in Florida I was challenged by her husband who claims to be an atheist. He told me that Jesus never claimed to be God incarnate, and that Jesus was only a man like anyone else. I didn't know what to say to him, so I gave him a terribly inadequate answer that I know did not help him. I feel bad about this and guess I really failed in witnessing. What could I have said?

Dear Failure-in-Witnessing,

Every one of us are failures at times, but God can turn every failure into a positive learning experience. Without the unsatisfactory confrontation with your friend's husband, the challenge for you to search out the Scriptures might have been greatly delayed.

When I was speaking at a women's luncheon in Victoria, B.C., some years ago I, too, was challenged. A woman present kept ordering cocktail after cocktail from the bar while sitting at a table with the rest of the group. It seemed obvious that she had a problem, but the other women didn't know exactly what to do about it.

After the meeting, as I was praying with a number of women, I received word that a woman in the hotel bar and lounge wanted to speak to me. It was the same person. I guess she had slipped out of the meeting near the last. Like your friend's husband, she challenged me to prove that Jesus is God. Sad to say, I didn't have as much ammunition as I needed Scripture-wise, but I did explain that knowing Jesus as God incarnate (God made man) was not an intellectual matter but something that could only be experienced in the heart. If she really wanted to know who He was, she needed to ask Him to come in and cleanse and heal her life. Then He could truly reveal Himself to her. I talked and prayed with her and trust God she was helped. As soon as I returned home, I loaded up on ammunition and wrote the pertinent Scriptures on the subject in back of my small Bible which I carry with me. (I know most of them by heart now.)

As I studied, I found that Jesus most often spoke of Himself as the "Son of man," identifying Himself with humanity. It's true that He didn't Himself often speak of His Divinity, or show that He was God. He knew it was necessary for this recognition to come from others as the Father revealed it to them through the Holy Spirit. For example, Matthew tells how one day Jesus asked His disciples, "Whom do men say that I the Son of man am?" or, to put it in the vernacular, "What are people saying about Me nowadays?" "And they said: 'Some say you are John the Baptist; some Elijah; and others, Jeremiah, or one of the prophets' " (Matt. 16:13b-14).

Then Jesus asked another more personal question, one that every person has to answer, "But who do *you* say that I am?" Simon Peter came through with flying colors on this one: "Thou art the Christ, the Son of the living God." Jesus must have been thrilled with Peter's answer. "Blessed are you, Simon Barjonas," He said, "because flesh and blood did not reveal this to you, but My Father who is in heaven" (Matt. 16:15-17 NASB).

As soon as Peter made his confession that Jesus is the Christ, Jesus confirmed it, but He wanted it to come from Peter, and not from Himself. Peter was a test case, a forerunner of multitudes of people just like him who would receive eternal life through Jesus long after He had left the face of the earth. Here we find Jesus admitting to be *the* Son of God and in doing so, equating Himself with God. Later, Jesus received a similar confession from Nathanael (John 1:47-51).

On the other hand, Jesus did sometimes clearly claim or evidence His divinity. The Gospel of John has more about the divinity of Jesus than any of the others. In John 8, we find a significant debate between the unbelieving Jews and Jesus. Jesus is claiming that whoever believes on Him will never see death. He goes on to say, "Your father Abraham rejoiced to see my day; and he saw it, and was glad!" (John 8:56). This puzzled the Jews, who realized Jesus was a young man and Abraham had been dead for some two thousand years. Jesus then said words that threw them into a rage: "I assure you . . . before Abraham was born, I AM"(John 8:58 TAB). Here Jesus used the parallel of the ancient Hebrew name of God which was thought to be so sacred it was never to be uttered. In the context, it is obvious that Jesus was claiming to be God; otherwise, the Jews wouldn't have tried to kill Him.

Jesus often said to people, "Your sins are forgiven." Long before He ever raised anyone from the dead or was raised from the dead Himself, He did not hesitate to say, "I am the resurrection and the life" (John 11:25). He admitted to the woman at the well that He was the promised Messiah, the anointed One. Jesus not only claimed to know the truth, but to be the Truth, and Life itself. He said, "No one comes to the Father, but by me" (John 14:6). Also, 'I am the light of the world" (John 8:12). On the mount of transfiguration, His countenance was so radiant that Peter, James, and John couldn't look at Him; His divinity was being manifested to this chosen few.

When the soldiers came to the Garden of Gethsemane looking for Jesus to imprison and crucify Him, they couldn't recognize Him. The soldiers then asked which one was Jesus of Nazareth, and Jesus answered with two words: "I am," and all the soldiers fell backward to the ground (John 18:6).* Those must have been very powerful words! While the soldiers were lying on the ground, Jesus could have made a getaway, but He waited, letting them get up, brush themselves off, and proceed to arrest Him. He was willingly giving His life. This proved

*When a word is in italics in the KJV, that means it wasn't in the original manuscript but was added by the translators. So when it says, "I am he," it would in actuality read, "I am."

158

the words He said earlier, "No man takes My life from Me, but I lay it down of Myself" (John 10:18 au. para.).

Jesus' crucifixion was made certain when He appeared before the high priest, who badgered Him for not defending Himself and asked Him, "Are you the Christ—the Messiah, the Anointed One—the Son of the Blessed?" And Jesus said, "I AM; and you will (all) see the Son of man seated at the right hand of Power (the Almighty), and coming with the clouds of heaven" (Mark 14:61-62 TAB). The high priest tore his garments, cried "Blasphemy!" and condemned Him. It's obvious here that Jesus was claiming divinity.

The last account I want to bring to your attention is again found in John. This is the most complete confession about Jesus Christ in the Gospels. The other disciples had seen Jesus in His resurrection body, but "doubting" Thomas wasn't with them at the time. When he heard the news, he said, "Unless I am able to see the nail-scarred hands and touch them and put my hand into Jesus' side where He was speared—I will not believe" (John 20:25 au. para.). Eight days later, Jesus visited the disciples again. Knowing what Thomas had said in his unbelief, Jesus showed him His hands and side. Thomas then cried out, "My Lord and my God" (John 20:28). Jesus didn't say, "Oh no, Thomas, I'm just a man like you are." He accepted Thomas' act of worship.

It's interesting that this confession took place after the resurrection. I believe it's only after Jesus' resurrection that anyone *could* make such a confession. When Jesus rose from the dead, that very evening He breathed resurrection life into His waiting disciples, imparting a totally new kind of life to them. And so it is with us today as we receive Jesus, that we come from death to resurrection life and are able to make the same confession as Thomas, saying, "My Lord and my God." Jesus also said that we would be greatly blessed, because though we may not have seen Jesus physically as Thomas did, yet we have believed in Him and received Him.

There are a number of other Scriptures in the Epistles and Old Testament as well as the Gospels, which you can look up yourself, but if you have these major ones marked in your Bible you'll be better prepared for witnessing next time. Perhaps you might write your friend and her husband and share some of these Scriptures with them. Remember, however, a person can never intellectualize his or her way to God. It's not wrong to ask questions, but after they've been answered, faith must be exercised to receive Jesus Christ in order to know Him.

Explain that it's all right to be completely honest with God. I once heard of a man who prayed: "Oh, God, if there is a God, save my soul if I have a soul!" I'm sure if such a prayer were sincerely made, God would answer it. Your friend can pray an experimental prayer and say, "God, if You are real, and if You have a Son named Jesus, I invite Him to come into my life and make You real to me. Thank You. Amen." God will answer such prayers, so be prepared to have further correspondence with your friend's husband and lead him on to the Baptism with the Holy Spirit. P.T.L.

Prayer Life

Dear Rita,

I am in my early twenties, am married and have three children under five. What concerns me is that I never have time to pray like most of the people in my church do. Several of my friends get up before their families do and spend an hour in prayer and Bible study. They have prayer lists, and they pray faithfully for all the people on them. Just hearing about their schedules makes me feel so unspiritual. Am I fooling myself that this is an impossible goal for me? How much time should a Christian mother spend in prayer?

Dear Unspiritual,

I saw this motto recently: "Life is fragile, handle with prayer." That would be a good motto to stick onto the bumper of a car, a suitcase, or onto packages that need special handling. It would also be good to somehow stick onto our lives.

161

Yes, indeed, prayer is like the breath of the Christian's life. It is basically talking with God, communicating love and needs—of yourself and others. It is also listening, and receiving His direction.

Prayer shouldn't have to be such hard work. Often, the way people talk about prayer, they make it seem impossible for anyone but those who have joined the religious life of monasteries or convents to be real people of prayer. Others get together to read long prayer lists, but never take much time to just spontaneously talk to God. A prayer list can be a helpful reminder, but it should not be substituted for spontaneous prayer that follows the Lord's leading.

It is good to have a set time each day to devote to prayer and Scripture reading. Ten or fifteen minutes would be a practical goal to aim for in the beginning. However, when that time is interrupted, you can still have conversational prayer with God throughout the day. Formal prayers that can be read have their place, but prayer from the heart is something you can do anytime. Try talking to the Lord while you clean house, wash dishes, iron clothes, or drive to the grocery store. If you took all the opportunities to pray, even in your busy life, and added them up, you would probably find you're praying as much as your friends or perhaps more!

In my experience, spontaneous prayer wasn't easy, nor did I spend much time at it, until I received the Baptism with the Holy Spirit. At that time, I was so filled up with joy, that I began to spill over in praise to God in a language given to me by the Holy Spirit. This is what the Bible calls speaking in tongues or praying in the Spirit: "For if I pray in an unknown tongue, my spirit prays, but my understanding is unfruitful. What is it then? I will pray with the spirit, and I will pray with the understanding also: I will sing with the spirit, and I will sing with the understanding also" (I Cor. 14:14-15).

Speaking in tongues means trusting God with your speech in such simplicity that you pray beyond the limitations of your intellect. When we run out of our own words with which to communicate to God, we can just open our mouths and trust God to give us the words. This is a most refreshing way to pray in addition to praying in your own language. Since you won't have to think about what you're saying when you pray in tongues, you can easily be doing household tasks and other things at the same time. You can also sing in the Spirit, letting the Holy Spirit guide both the words and music, giving you a brand-new song.

Every Christian is also praying with or in the Spirit when he prays with his intellect, as it is only by the spirit (that innermost part of us where God dwells) that we can contact God at all. However, speaking in tongues is prayer one-hundred percent with the Spirit—not partially with the Spirit and partially with the mind—and is therefore more refreshing, so you will feel like praying more.

Another wonderful thing about praying in tongues is that when you feel impressed to pray for a friend or loved one and don't know exactly how to pray, you can pray in the Spirit, knowing that the Holy Spirit will guide you to pray a perfect prayer (Rom. 8:26).

How much time should a Christian mother spend in prayer? The Bible says, "Praying always with all prayer and supplication in the Spirit" (Eph. 6:18); "Pray without ceasing" (I Thess. 5:17); "In everything by prayer and supplication with thanksgiving let your requests be made known to God" (Phil. 4:6). Only by praying conversationally and one hundred percent in the Spirit is this possible.

I believe that even as you sleep, your spirit is praying; otherwise it would be impossible to pray always. It might be good to pray before retiring at night, "Lord, even as I rest, I want my spirit to be in communication and fellowship with You." This may sound like an awfully easy kind of prayer life, lying there in bed peacefully praying within. There are times when God will call you to intercede for needs of others, which takes more effort, but basically speaking, prayer should be as easy as breathing. As the psalmist David says, "Let everything that hath breath praise the Lord" (Ps. 150:6). If you're breathing, then you should be praying and praising God.

Praying with Children

Dear Rita,

One of my children, a little girl five years old, is asking a lot of questions about Jesus. She seems especially interested in the Crucifixion, and wants me to read her that story from our Bible storybook, over and over. It seems to make her sad, but she loves it just the same. Is this normal? What should I tell her about the Lord?

Dear Mother,

Little children are much more ready to hear and understand about God, and about Jesus and what He did for us, than we imagine they are. It is not at all unusual for very young children to take a deep interest in spiritual things, and especially to be fascinated by the Person and Name of Jesus and everything about Him, including the Crucifixion. Somehow, they seem instinctively to know the importance of it. It is surprising the grasp that young children sometimes have of even very deep theological matters.

While my husband and I were holding a mission in the Episcopal Cathedral in Jacksonville, Florida, several years ago, a sweet little six-year-old girl, the daughter of one of the leading laymen, came to me. This youngster had already received Jesus as her Savior and been baptized in the Holy Spirit, and was telling her playmates about Jesus. She brought with her a five-year-old friend. She wanted me to help her meet Jesus. The little girls and I knelt down at the altar rail, and the very first thing the five-year-old asked me was to explain the Trinity.* I wasn't quite expecting this, but I gulped and, trying to make it as simple as possible, I said, "God the Father is God above you; God the Son is God with you; and God the Holy Spirit is God in you." I was relieved when the child was gravely thoughtful for a moment, and then said, "Oh, I see." Then I went on to explain how God comes to live in us by His Holy Spirit when we ask Jesus to wash away our sins and come into our hearts and give us new life. I used the very familiar passage of Revelation 3:20 and explained that Jesus is knocking at the heart's door of every man, woman, girl, or boy, but that He can't come in unless they open the door. I explained how God had purposely made our heart's door with only one handle, and that one on the inside. The little girl cocked her head to one side, and said, "I think I hear Him knocking!"

"Well, just ask Him to come in."

She quickly said, "Come in, Jesus!"

Simple, wasn't it? Yet from experience with other cases, I know that Jesus did come in, and that that little child's life will not be the same, because the Holy Spirit is now living in her. Never assume that a child is too young to understand the things of God. I have known of children being baptized in the Holy Spirit, speaking in other tongues, as young

*The word, "Trinity," is not in the Bible, but the picture of God in His tri-unity is certainly there. The word, "Trinity," puts in a capsule what the Bible says all the way through.

as four years of age. We do not go around encouraging very young children to be baptized in the Holy Spirit, but sometimes it happens spontaneously. It is not uncommon to have parents report that while they were praying in the Spirit at home, they suddenly realized that one of the younger children was joining in.

When should you tell your child about Jesus? If your child is old enough to know that she loves her mother and father, she is old enough to love Jesus. And if she is showing an interest in spiritual things, you should share just as much as she is ready to listen to. Every youngster is different, but they usually are much more interested and ready to hear about God than we expect them to be.

After all, the Gospel, the good news of Jesus, is simple, isn't it? Paul was concerned about his friends at Corinth lest they should lose the "simplicity which is in Christ." And it is just as simple for adults as for little children. One Sunday on our radio broadcast, Dennis was telling our listeners how simple it is to become a Christian; he quoted the Scripture, "Believe on the Lord Jesus Christ and you will be saved." A listener called up and took him to task for making it too simple. He hadn't given a thorough explanation about the Blood of Jesus—he hadn't explained about the Atonement. Dennis was a bit crestfallen as we left for lunch—perhaps, he felt, he did make it too "simplistic." Then, as we waited for a traffic light to change in downton Seattle, a large panel truck drove slowly in front of us, and on its side in large letters was written: BELIEVE IN THE LORD JESUS CHRIST AND YOU WILL BE SAVED! We both got the message, and began to laugh and praise God. He often picks unusual ways to speak to His kids!

Certainly, it's important to realize that God forgives us our sins, not just once, but many times, and that we need to confess our sins to Him. It's important to understand, as much as we can, what His death on Calvary meant in terms of defeating the enemy, and cleansing us from our sins by His precious Blood. It's important to understand these things as fully as we are able, but the most important thing is that we "call upon the Name of the Lord." If we say, "Help me, Lord Jesus!", He will hear us, and rescue us, and be our Good Shepherd.

What a privilege it is to be a mother. One of the most important things you can do is to help lead your children to Jesus Christ just as you have been doing, and then to pray with them to invite Jesus to come into their hearts. Hopefully, your husband will want to help pray with them, too. Then, when they are old enough to desire the Baptism with the Holy Spirit, it would be important to pray with them for this, too.

If the first six years of a child's life are filled with the love and security a mother and father can give, in addition to Christian upbringing and experience of Christ, it will have the best start possible. Then you can claim the Scripture in Proverbs 22:6, "Train up a child in the way he should go"—that's

your part—"and when he is old, he will not depart
from it"—that's God's part. Since you've done your
part, God will certainly do His. Happy mothering!

Guess who moved?

God's Presence

Dear Rita,

I have been a baptized-in-the-Spirit Christian for several years and it has been great. But for the last six months, the joy and power in my life seem to have vanished into thin air like a puff of smoke. I'm sure the Spirit-filled life is not supposed to be the struggle mine has become. What's gone wrong?

Dear Struggling Christian,

I heard a story some time ago of a husband and wife who were driving along in their car. She was sitting way over near her door, while he was in the driver's seat. She was complaining to her husband that he was not as affectionate or interested in her as he used to be. He finally looked at her and said just two words: "Who moved?"

Ask yourself the same question about Jesus. He has never left the driver's seat, but are you sitting as close beside Him as you used to? Jesus said, "I will never leave you, nor forsake you" (Heb. 13:5). Even bumper stickers have now taken up this thought with the words, "Guess who moved?"

A young person came to me with a question like yours, and the Lord inspired me to ask her, "What were you doing *then* that you're not doing *now?*" She thought a moment and got the point. You could reverse that and get additional insight. "What are you doing *now* that you weren't doing *then?*"

In his book, *High Adventure*, George Otis compares the Christian life to a car driving up a very steep mountain, but having no brakes! In other words, a Christian must be moving on with God or he will be sliding backward.

After we receive the Baptism with the Holy Spirit, the Lord Jesus is able to reveal in our lives old habit patterns and psychological hang-ups that need to be changed. It is, as John said, a baptism with the Holy Ghost *and* with *fire* (Luke 3:16). This may be what you are experiencing. God wants you to go on with Him, but there are areas that He won't put up with any longer. As you are obedient in letting Him correct those areas in your life which hinder your fellowship with God, that wonderful love-relationship will return, more heightened than ever. Ask the Lord to remove any blindness that would keep you from seeing a need to change.

The greatest experience we can have in this life is to know the loving presence of God. *Nothing* is worth losing that—for even a short time. Missing the sense of His presence and fellowship is a spiritual thermometer built into the center of our beings. It's a warning to the Christian that something is wrong—so that we can make it right.

Let Jesus take the struggle out of your life. Stick close to the Driver!

Childbearing

Dear Rita,

What does the Scripture mean when it says a woman shall be saved through childbearing? It sounds like unless a woman bears children, she can't be given eternal life. I know this must not be the proper interpretation, but since I'm childless, this verse has bothered me

Dear Bothered,

This is a good example of why it is important not to base a doctrine on one or two lone Scriptures lifted out of the Bible. One cult I know of actually teaches something like what you cited.

For a teaching to be valid, it must be upheld throughout the whole of the Scriptures in the Old and New Testaments. Some time ago I read a statement about proper interpretation of Scripture, which registered with me: "Look for the truth that makes all Scriptures compatible (not contradictory to one another) rather than the truth that makes a Scripture compatible to your way of thinking."

Let's look at the verse to which you are referring. "But she shall be saved through the childbearing, if they remain in faith and love, and holiness and self-control" (I Tim. 2:15 free translation NGT). Obviously this cannot mean that women are saved, not by the blood of Jesus, but by their own suffering in bearing children. This would contradict all the rest of the Scripture, and would bring us right back to a doctrine of being saved by our own efforts, making up for our own sins. We know that this cannot be the meaning of the passage.

What then does it mean? Many commentators and translators take it to mean simply, "She will be brought safely through the dangers and pains of childbirth." The word for "saved" in Greek means "kept, protected," as well as referring to spiritual salvation. A part of the suffering that the woman brought on herself by her rebellion against God was the pain and danger of childbirth, and so Paul may be saying that by faith in Jesus, she will be protected and brought safely through. But the little Greek word *dia*, "through," can be used in several ways. It can mean "through" in the sense of "during," and it can also mean "by means of."

Note that the passage speaks not just of "child-bearing," but of "*the* childbearing." May not this refer to the great "Child-Bearing"—that is, Mary bearing Jesus?* Whether or not this was what Paul had

*Some commentators have thought so. A footnote to this verse in the New English Bible reads, in part, "*Or* saved through the Birth of the Child." The Amplified Bible renders the passage, "[Saved indeed] through the Child-bearing, that is, by the birth of the [divine] Child."

174

in mind when he wrote the passage, it is meaningful to interpret it in this way. The Holy Spirit will often give a deeper and broader meaning to a Scripture than perhaps even the original writer saw. This is quite common in the prophets of the Old Testament—what they wrote has a broader meaning than they would have perceived as they wrote.

We know that the Bible from beginning to end teaches that Jesus Christ was *the* only Child born into this world who would be able to save anyone. It also says "she" shall be saved—speaking *initially* of one woman, then of the many other women to follow. Mary, the mother of Jesus, was saved not only by being the channel to bring the Savior Christ into the world but also by accepting Him as her Lord and Savior. Many children had to be born into the world to prepare the way for Jesus Christ to be born of Mary; in this sense only, were women saved by means of childbearing. They, too, had to accept Jesus as their Lord and Savior to be rescued from their sins.

Isn't God's grace beautiful? A woman, Eve, caused Adam's fall, and sin came into the world; and through another woman, Mary, thousands of years later, the One Who alone could save all who came to Him was born.

God's grace and love are powerfully demonstrated in the story of "the woman of the city who was a sinner," probably a prostitute. One evening while Jesus was having dinner at a Pharisee's home, this woman somehow was admitted and began to weep all over His feet and to dry them with her hair. Then she anointed them with expensive sweet-smelling ointment. Some believe the ointment to be the very perfume she had formerly used to lure men to herself. This very act of pouring out the ointment in her alabaster box, showed she was turning from her former way of life. When Jesus was criticized for permitting such an action, He said to the self-righteous Pharisee: "Her sins, which are many, are forgiven; for she loved much: but to whom little is forgiven, the same loveth little" (Luke 7:47).

Perhaps women who have acknowledged their crucial part in the fall of man realize how much they have been forgiven, and so as this woman did, they love much in return.

Like you, I have borne no children. But I am sure of my salvation. Some Scripture that may be a blessing to you is found in Isaiah 54:1-3a: "Sing, O barren, thou that didst not bear; break forth into singing, and cry aloud, thou that didst not travail with child: for more are the children of the desolate than the children of the married wife, saith the Lord. Enlarge the place of thy tent, and let them stretch forth the curtains of thine habitations: spare not lengthen thy cords, and strengthen thy stakes; For thou shalt break forth on the right hand and on the left."

I take the spiritual interpretation of this to mean that even if you don't have your own flesh and blood children, yet God promises that you can have scores of spiritual children by leading souls to Jesus. What a privilege it is to be able to help populate heaven! As an apple tree bears apples, so the Christian life should bear the fruit of other Christians. Don't be childless, but be as a fruitful tree bringing many into the kingdom.

MINISTRY

I'm not disputing; I just disagree with you.

Women Speaking in Church

Dear Rita,

It has always seemed to me that Paul is contradicting himself in one particular place in the Scripture. It's in I Corinthians 14:34-35 where Paul admonishes the Corinthian men not to permit their wives to speak in the church but says they must remain absolutely silent. Yet a few chapters prior to this, Paul gave counsel about the Corinthian women being under proper headship, but implied that these same women may pray and prophesy. The Scripture says prophecy is the greatest gift with which to edify *the church,* and here Paul says women are permitted to minister this gift. How can they do it if they are not allowed to speak in church? This really has made me curious to know if Paul forgot what he had said previously.

Dear Curious-to-Know,

I understand what you mean about these Scriptures and have talked to other women who were similarly puzzled. Let's look at them: "Let your women keep silence in the churches: for it is not permitted for them to speak; but they are commanded to be under obedience, as the law* also says. And if they will learn anything, let them ask their husbands

---

*This is a reference to Genesis 3:16: "Thy desire shall be to thy husband, and he shall rule over thee."

at home: for it is a shame for women to speak in the church" (I Cor. 14:34-35).

This was based on a Jewish ordinance which stated that women were not permitted to teach in the assemblies, or even to ask questions. Such was their condition till the time of the Gospel, when according to the prediction of Joel, the Spirit of God was to be poured out on the women as well as the men, that they may "prophesy." That they did prophesy is indeed evident from Paul's statement in chapter eleven, verse five: "But every woman that prays or prophesies with her head uncovered dishonours her head."

It is obvious from the context that what Paul is attempting to correct here is directed to those particular women asking questions and "dictating" in the assemblies. It had always been permitted to any man to ask questions, to object, attempt to refute, in the synagogue; but this liberty was not allowed to the woman. Paul confirms his belief in this practice in verse thirty-five where he explains the preceding verse which orders them to *keep silence* and ask questions at home. (It seems to me that verse thirty-five is the solution to verse thirty-four.) He felt it was indecorous for women to be contending with men in public assemblies, on points of doctrine, and so forth. All that the apostle opposes here is their questioning, finding fault, disputing, in the Christian church, as the Jewish men were permitted to do in their synagogues.*

*Adam Clarke's Commentary, abridged by Ralph Earle (Grand Rapids, Mich.: Baker Book House, 1967), p. 1119.

"For it is a shame for women to speak in the church." The Jews would not permit a woman to read in the synagogue, though a male servant or even a child had this permission. But here at the beginning of the Church, the apostle must be referring to irregular and disorderly conduct which proved that the women were not "under obedience" or submitted to authority over them.*

In Old Testament times, as people began to know God, the attitude toward women began to change. As Judaism blossomed into Christianity, women were given greater respect and liberty than ever before. In the early days of the Church, as women were emancipated from complete subservience to men, some carried their freedom too far. In their enthusiasm, they began to ignore what they had learned in the law. Also, the average woman had little education, and with her new freedom and newfound faith must have taken a great interest in the Scriptures. She was now motivated to learn. Bible scholars have suggested that since the men would be sitting on one side of the room and women on the other, the women would be calling back and forth to their husbands, asking them questions and disagreeing with them.

Paul was striving for decency and order. Decency here means plain old good manners. Women, not being accustomed to public situations, were bound to make mistakes.

I think another big problem was that women, generally, are more verbal than men, and usually

*Ibid., p. 1120.

more interested in details. When they got "turned on," it must have been hard to "turn them off." You've heard the old saying, "If you want to get some news out, telephone, telegraph, or tell-a-woman." There may be more truth in this than we've realized, or like to admit! I saw a recent magazine article stating that a professor in England has measured the velocity of the English spoken there, and finds that men speak an average of 76 words a minute, while women talk at a rate of 105 words per minute. This would be great for witnessing, but could work havoc if the speech of women in the Church was undisciplined.

Although the situation of the Corinthian women is different from ours in many ways, Paul's instruction does have relevance for women today. It says to me that since women find it easier to speak, they should be even more careful than men to speak from the spirit and not from the soul. If they do this, they will speak less, and when they do speak, it will be pure and a blessing to all. Incidentally, both of the references you mentioned have one thing in common—in them, God is reminding women to be under the protective covering of their husbands' headship.*

Since women are told they may prophesy, we should be knowledgeable on this subject. Paul said that prophecy is the greatest gift with which to edify the Church. It is supernatural speech that "edifies, exhorts, or comforts," and sometimes tells of things

*Headship is discussed on pp. 25-96.

to come. Living in the Spirit, walking in the Spirit, and speaking in the Spirit is good preparation for letting God use you in the gift of prophecy. This gift occurs when believers speak the mind of God, by the inspiration of the Holy Spirit. It is supernatural speech in a known language; it doesn't come by pre-meditation or study. It is not teaching, and it is not witnessing. It is not looking in a crystal ball or telling fortunes.

On the Day of Pentecost, when the first Christians received the power of the Holy Spirit, Peter explained to the onlookers by quoting from the prophet Joel, "And it shall come to pass in the last days, saith God, I will pour out of my Spirit upon all flesh: and your sons *and your daughters shall prophesy,* and your young men shall see visions, and your old men shall dream dreams: And on my servants and on my *handmaidens* I will pour out in those days of my Spirit: and *they shall prophesy*" (Acts 2:17-18). These are pretty positive words about women prophesying. The outpouring of the Holy Spirit at Pentecost and ever since then, empowers women and men equally to bring prophecy from the Lord.

If any woman wants to bless others through the gift of prophecy, she should study the Scriptures and read books by charismatic teachers on the subject so that her ministry will be properly ordered. She should be in a solid prayer fellowship that believes in the gifts and welcomes them. And she must be under her husband's and/or minister's headship.

Let's look at some of the women who prophesied

in the New Testament. A good example of prophecy is the one that Mary brought concerning the honor God gave her in choosing her to be the mother of the Messiah (Luke 1:46-55). Anna, too, had a special ministry. She was called a prophetess because God gave her His words for His people. She was in the temple of Jerusalem when the infant Jesus was brought there to be presented to the Lord. She spoke about Jesus to others in the temple and proclaimed who He was. No doubt, she did this by the inspiration of the Holy Spirit, so it was a prophetic utterance (Luke 2:36-38). We read also of Philip the evangelist's four unmarried daughters who all were known for their ministry in prophecy (Acts 21:8-9). They must have spoken prophetically in the Church and been submitted to Philip and other leaders of the synagogue they attended. Daughters like these must have added much to Philip's already exciting life!

When a woman has properly prepared herself and is not domineering or "headless," her ministry of prophecy can be a real blessing. She should not share the gift so often that she is doing a frequent solo, but should be sure to let the men and other women have their share in ministry.

No, I'm sure Paul was not absentminded. Doubtless he did not mean to deny women all opportunity for speaking under the inspiration of the Holy Spirit or to imply that it's shameful for a woman to speak in church.* However, at all times,

---

*Charles M. Laymon, ed., *The Interpreter's One-Volume Commentary* New York, N. Y.: Abingdon, 1971), p. 809.

let's be careful that we speak from the Spirit—especially when we are speaking in public.

Here's a good recipe to add to your kitchen files: "Let your speech be always with grace, seasoned with salt, that you may know how you ought to answer every man" (Col. 4:6).

Women Teaching Men

Dear Rita,

My pastor has asked me to conduct a six-weeks' Bible study in our adult Bible class. I have had a teaching ministry for a number of years now. Recently, however, I have read some strong articles and heard tapes by several well-known teachers stating that women are *never* supposed to teach men on religious topics under any circumstances. Who is right—my pastor or these others? I truly want to do what God wants me to. What advice can you give me?

Dear Teacher,

The Scripture most often quoted against women teaching men is found in I Timothy 2:11-14: "Let a woman learn in quietness in all subjection; but a woman to teach I do not allow, nor to exercise authority over man, but to be in quietness; for Adam first was formed, then Eve; and Adam was not deceived; but the woman, having been deceived, in transgression has become."* Marshall's translation of Nestle's Greek text says, "But I do not permit a woman to teach nor to exercise authority *of* a man" (I Tim. 2:12 NGT). In other words, the woman is not to try to take the place of the man nor to act as though she has the same authority.

An Australian commentator suggests that verse twelve might read, "I suffer not a woman to teach authority [authoritatively], nor to usurp authority over the man." This, he says, does no violence to the Greek syntax. It sounds much like Marshall's translation of the Nestle text.

The word "usurp" as used here and in some other translations helps to clarify the Scripture. *The American Heritage Dictionary* describes usurp this way: "To seize and hold, as the power, position, or rights of another, by force and without legal right or authority."

The passage of Scripture in I Timothy actually brings up *two* questions: How much authority does a woman have in the Church? Can a woman teach adults in a co-ed situation?

In God's particular plan for authority in the Church and home, there is no question about the man having the final authority. Although God chose

*Berry, *The Interlinear Greek-English New Testament.*

Deborah, the prophetess, to be a judge in Israel, women in government were rare, and were probably used only when there was not a qualified man available. There is no example of a woman priest in the Old Testament or a woman elder or bishop in the New Testament, nor as head of a normal home situation. The woman was not created to have the final authority over the man within the Church or the home. This is not to say that a woman is not as capable as a man, but simply that this is not God's regular order for the woman, as she has another role to fill which is uniquely hers. It is for the woman's protection and for the preservation of a healthy church family structure that this order was established.*

What does it mean to teach? Teaching means simply to impart knowledge or to give instruction. Every time a woman leads a person to Jesus Christ as Savior and/or Baptizer, she is teaching or imparting knowledge.

The basic reason for Paul's caution about women teaching men was that the woman was the first to be deceived about spiritual things. Apparently the man did not fall into sin because of deception, as Eve did, but by willful disobedience, perhaps because he desired to be at one with his wife. Most likely if she had not tried to answer Satan's theological questions all by herself, but had waited to talk it over

---

*We must recognize of course that there are women who are capably carrying out leadership of churches. We are not trying to detract from or criticize them. Their ministries, however, are "valid but irregular," to use the traditional theological term, and not to be set up as the norm.

with Adam, Eve would have had a greater measure of protection.

Although I Timothy taken at face value says no to women teaching men, the Bible as a whole seems to say something quite different. Basing doctrine on one or two Scriptures and ignoring the many other examples where women taught with men present is not a sound principle.

Let us look at some actual examples in Scripture: When the woman of Samaria came to believe in Jesus as Messiah, she went into the city and told the men about Jesus and convinced them of His reality as the Christ: "The woman then left her waterpot, and went her way into the city, and said to the men, Come, see a man, which told me all things that ever I did: is not this the Christ? Then they went out of the city and came to him. And many of the Samaritans of that city believed on him for the saying of the woman" (John 4:28-30, 39a).

Note that she shared and talked with the men but did not try to set herself up as an authority over them. Here we find a Samaritan woman being the one Jesus allowed to be first to declare Him as Messiah to the Gentile world!* All Gentiles can be thankful for the effective witness of this woman.

Romans 16 has the longest list of commendable

---

*Samaritans were not half Jew and half Gentile, but they were Assyrians or Gentiles: "Such were the Samaritans of our Lord's day; a people distinct from the Jews, though lying in the very midst of the Jews, a people preserving their identity, though seven centuries had rolled away since they had been brought from Assyria by Esarhaddon." William Smith, *Smith's Bible Dictionary* (Old Tappan, N. J.: Revell, 1967), p. 598.

women in the New Testament. There are at least nine listed: Phebe, Priscilla, Mary, Tryphena, Tryphosa, Persis, Rufus' mother (also like a mother to Paul), Julia, and Nereus' sister.

Phebe in being listed first in this chapter is given honorable mention. "Now I commend to you Phebe our sister, being also a minister* of the church—in Cenchrea, in order that you may receive her in (the) Lord worthily of the saints, and may stand by her in whatever things she may have need of; for indeed she became a protectress** of many and of myself also" (Rom. 16:1-2 free translation from NGT). Phebe had the title of a deacon—that is the Greek meaning for "minister" in this verse—indicating she held office in the Church (I Tim. 3:8-13). She was also a helper of the apostles and undoubtedly submitted to their leadership.

Phebe was the one Paul trusted to deliver his important letter or epistle into the hands of the Roman Christians. Paul had not yet visited Rome, so the person chosen to represent him must have been thoroughly responsible. It wasn't exactly an easy journey in those days. Our debt to Phebe is great; had she failed, we might not have the Book of Romans in our Bible.

---

*This is the Greek word *diakonos* or "deacon" (not deaconess), which means, "One who executes the command of another." At the present time in the Episcopal or Anglican Church, The Order of the Diaconate is the one existing ordained ministry for women.

**Succourer or protectress is "a word of dignity, . . . and indicates the high esteem with which she was regarded." W. E. Vine, *Expository Dictionary of New Testament Words* (London: Oliphants, 1940) p. 88.

191

Priscilla, the second person mentioned in this list, was another outstanding woman. Tertullian, one of the early fathers, spoke of her as "the holy Prisca, who preached the gospel." She traveled and worked very closely with her husband, Aquila. They probably had a Christian assembly in their home. Paul lived with them for a while, and worked together with them in the trade of tentmaking. When he writes to them, he often puts Priscilla's name first, which was not the custom. Paul had a high respect for Priscilla and her ministry.

In Acts 18:24-26 we find Aquila and Priscilla ministering to an apostle. The Book of Acts tells us that Apollos was a wonderful man of God, an eloquent speaker, powerful in the Scriptures and the things concerning Jesus, but he understood only the baptism of John. It goes on to say, "And this man began to speak boldly in the synagogue. And hearing him, Priscilla and Aquila took him and more accurately explained the way of God to him" (free translation from NGT).

It is very likely that they taught Apollos about the Baptism in the Holy Spirit and the gifts of the Spirit and prayed with him for these blessings. Priscilla must have done quite a bit of the teaching, and it is even thought by some that the ministry to Apollos was initiated by her. No doubt Aquila and Priscilla had great respect and love for one another. It is also obvious that the teaching of this couple was under Paul's headship. Paul was in loving fellowship with his two friends to the end of his life on earth.

The Scripture tells of many women who worked closely with Paul in his ministry. In Philippians 4:2 there are others named, and Paul says, "I ask you, true yokefellow, to help these women [Euodia* and Syntyche] who worked hard together with me in the gospel [good news]; with Clement, too, and the rest of my co-workers (Phil. 4:3 free translation from NGT). Whoever was the yokefellow with Paul must have been a yokefellow, too, with these women. In verse two, the reference to Euodia and Syntyche and their problems is extremely revealing in regard to women's ministry in those days. Paul does not say to these two, "Stop teaching! What's the idea of you women teaching?" He simply says, "Please work together; be of the same mind in the Lord." This sounds as if Paul recognized them as having considerable authority in what they were saying and doing. It is very doubtful that Euodia and Syntyche were doing only such things as waiting on tables, as they "worked with Paul in the gospel."

In John 20, Mary Magdalene met Jesus at the tomb and He told her, "Go to my brethren, and say unto them, I ascend unto my Father and your Father; and to my God and your God" (John 20:17b). Here and in Matthew 28:1-10 Jesus is again, as with the woman at the well, encouraging a woman to go and share the glad tidings. This is doubly interesting because, in those days, a woman's witness was not acceptable in court. Jesus knew the prejudices of

---

*In the KJV, Euodias should be spelled Euodia for the feminine form of the name.

His day, but He still chose to have a woman as the first witness to His resurrection.

Psalm 68:11 speaks specifically of women being sent to proclaim the Gospel. This truth was hidden from me until recently, as I usually read Psalms in the KJV translation where the word "company" has been inserted in place of "women." The literal Hebrew says, "The Lord gave the word, and the number of women that published the good news was a tremendous army." The Book of Common Prayer uses the Coverdale version of the Psalms, which is older than the King James: "The Lord gave the word, great was the company of women that bare the tidings."

Throughout the Bible, men, of course, are commissioned to proclaim the good news *to all*, but it is encouraging to find such Scriptures in which God specifically approves of women sharing the good news with all.

There are two extreme views about woman's role, and place in the Body of Christ. Liberal ministers have said that the Scriptures relating to women have *no* bearing on them today. On the other side of the picture, there are the legalists who take one or two verses of Scripture out of context and build a theory on them, ignoring the rest of the Bible. In the first case, the woman is left without any guidelines for her life. In the second, she is beaten down and brought into legalistic bondage.

Let's look at this second attitude carried to the extreme. If women could never impart any religious knowledge to men, all songs written by women would have to be removed from Christian songbooks. Christian poetry and other literature by great Christians such as Dorothy Sayers, Evelyn Underhill, Hanna Whitall Smith, Fanny Crosby, and a host of others would be off-limits for men. Men would have to turn off radios and television when a woman might possibly share some Christian information. They would have to stop their ears in a charismatic meeting if a woman prophesied, because there is often a word of knowledge or wisdom imparting information, which is interwoven in prophecy. Women would never be able to witness to men about Jesus. A wife could not share with her husband any inspired thoughts she received from the Lord during her prayer and Bible-reading time. He could share with her, but she could not share with him. This idea gets quite ridiculous, but to be consistent with such teachings, this is where one would end.

I don't think this legalism is what Paul had in mind, as it would contradict the many other Scriptures I've just cited. His real concern, I believe, could be summed up in three statements:

1. The woman should know her role and be yielded to the proper authority.
2. When the woman teaches,* she is to be submitted to male leadership and not try to usurp the place of the man or to attempt to rule over him.

---

*The word "teach" could also have meant in Paul's day and time, "to disciple," to develop a group of followers. Paul would not have wanted a woman to rule over a number of male disciples.

3. The woman should not teach a doctrine different from that given to the Church.*

If a married woman is submitted to her husband and to her pastor, and they want her to teach in a Bible class composed of men and women, I believe the Scripture supports her doing so.** The minister should also know what she's going to be teaching, and the basic premises should be submitted to him for approval as they go along.

My answer to your question is in full agreement with my own husband who happens also to be my minister. I know God will guide you in your decision. After all, it's *God* who raises up teachers, and He will see to it that His Word is proclaimed.

For Women Only

Dear Rita,

Since childhood, the Scriptures have been an important part of my life. After high school, I at-

---

Didasko is the Greek word most often used in the New Testament when speaking of teaching. *Heterodidaskaleo* is the Greek word meaning "to teach a different doctrine" or to "teach otherwise," what is contrary to the faith.

**If she is unmarried or widowed, her pastor should approve her teaching this class

tended and graduated from Bible college with honors. It is quite natural that I should have taught a number of Bible classes through the years, both women's classes and coeducational ones.

Recently, through hearing other teachers, I've come to the conclusion that the scriptural admonition for women *not* to teach men should be heeded. Since I have taken this stand, my husband has begun to step forward in the area of Bible teaching, where I'm afraid I have overshadowed him in the past. At the same time, I am still continuing to have an effective ministry.

I've been so convinced on this point of women teaching only women that if a man comes into my class, I have trouble continuing to teach. Am I carrying my conviction too far? I have been criticized for my attitude, and yet, don't I have the Scriptures on my side? I would like to know what you think about it.

Dear Convinced,

It sounds to me as if you have been following the Lord's will for your life. The results certainly prove it. Often, I have found that men feel spiritually inferior to their wives; and when this is so, they step back and let the women take the lead. This is one reason why church congregations are so often made up of women and children on Sunday morning while husbands are out fishing or golfing.

I'm glad to see, especially in the charismatic renewal, that men are beginning to fill the churches and take their place as spiritual leaders. Women whose husbands have been lagging behind might well follow your example and take a step or two backward so their husbands may catch up.

On the other hand, I do believe that some of the current teaching is a bit exaggerated. It is true that Scripture can be cited that says women should not teach men; on the other hand, other Scriptures seem to indicate that women did do general teaching and were accepted and respected as leaders in the Church. We cannot go by proof texts on such things, but must consider the whole of the Scripture. There seems to be no question but that it is better, wherever possible, for women regularly to teach women and men regularly to teach men, but if we make this a legalistic requirement, surely we are putting the people of God under bondage again.

At times women will want to meet separately to talk about things that relate particularly to them. There are topics which are specifically for women, and it would be inappropriate for men to be present; in other circumstances, however, for a woman leader to feel she should not teach if men are present would seem to be questioning the very authority she desires to obey. Surely your husband or your minister, under whose headship you are, should feel free to attend your class to see what you are teaching and how the class is progressing.

Your present position is no doubt best for you, but to teach all women to follow your convictions exactly would be unfortunate. Women whose husbands would not be threatened by their wives on occasion teaching co-ed classes would not have to follow your particular guidance. Each person's life is unique, and each woman must seek the Lord's will for her own situation.

Often people are like a weighing scale. The scale tips up high on one extreme position; then, that's exchanged for another opinion, and the scale tips up on the opposite side. Extremes should be guarded against; we should aim for a balanced position.

It sounds to me as if you are to be commended in your work. The saying, "If you're not doing anything worthwhile you won't make any mistakes," is relevant here. It takes a mature person to accept helpful criticism and profit by it. Apply what you can, and then get on with the work that is before you.

What Women Can Do

Dear Rita,

I'm tired of hearing about all the things a woman can't do in the Church. How about some ideas on what she *can* do? I desire to serve the Lord but just don't know what is considered a proper or fitting ministry for a woman.

Dear Desiring-to-Serve,

To begin with, let's define what the Church is. When Jesus challenged His first followers with the idea of building His Church, He didn't point them to a pile of bricks and bags of mortar and say, "Now, get going." The Church is not a building, but a group of gathered professed believers.

The word "church" comes from the word *ekklesia* which means "called out of." Not only that, but we're called *together* for fellowship, up-building, refreshing, and nourishment, so we can be better ministers in our homes and to the world.

Women sometimes feel that they are not given important tasks to do because many churches try to keep them out of administrative capacities. Yet, the apostles had seven men appointed to take over the administrative work so that they could give themselves to "the Word of God, and prayer." Even these men did not stick to administration, for we find both Stephen and Philip, soon after, proclaiming the Word of God. So "the Word of God, and prayer" are the areas of primary importance, let's see what women can do in these and other ways.

You can pray. Many women head up church or home prayer chains, which are available to pray for urgent needs around the clock. If women would pray more and talk less about problems in the Church, greater things would be accomplished to build God's

Kingdom. Luke in his Gospel record tells about Anna, an elderly woman who was not only a prophetess but spent much of her life in prayer (Luke 2:36-38). She had the privilege of being one of the first to recognize Jesus after His birth and to acknowledge Him publicly as the Messiah.

Some women feel especially called to visit and pray for the sick in hospitals. Most ministers have more people than they can care for, and if you prepare yourself for this work, you can lighten his load. You might purchase a portable tape recorder and obtain some good faith-building tapes to leave with the sick person. Books on healing would also be helpful.

A woman may manifest the gift of prophecy in the Church or any of the other gifts of the Holy Spirit. She should study the Scriptures concerning the gifts so they will be manifested according to God's divine order.

In Titus 2, the mature or older women are given a number of directions, and two of them concern teaching. They are to be:

1. Teachers of good things.
2. Teachers of the young women:
   a. to be sober
   b. to love their husbands
   c. to love their children
   d. to be discreet (having a judicious reserve in speech or behavior)
   e. to be chaste (virtuous, pure)

    f. to be keepers at home (especially when they have small children)

    g. to be good

    h. to be obedient to their own husbands

Many women are Sunday school teachers or invite children to their homes to tell them about the Lord. This is an area of great need and fulfillment.

You could start a Bible coffee fellowship in your neighborhood. There are many good Bible studies to assist you in this. A woman may also teach co-ed Bible classes when asked by the pastor of the church and, if she is married, her husband approves.

Your talent may be in music. You may sing in the choir, be the soloist, or even the choir directress. You may play the organ, piano, or other instruments to God's glory. Many young people today are asked to accompany group singing with their guitars and tambourines (timbrels is the Bible name).

A woman may be used to lead the congregation or small groups in singing. It is surprising how often in the Old Testament God chose women to lead His people in singing praises and in worship. Isaiah 12:6 says: "Cry out and shout, thou inhabitant of Zion: for great is the Holy One of Israel in the midst of thee." That the Hebrew word is actually the feminine form is borne out by the Amplified Bible's rendering, "Cry aloud and shout joyfully, you *women* . , . of Zion."

Counselors are also in demand. A counselor needs to know how to lead a person to Jesus, how to pray for the Baptism with the Holy Spirit, and to pray for healing in soul and body. She should also be informed in the area of marriage counseling.* More complicated psychological cases can be referred to your minister.

Just a brief word about administrative duties in the Church. Some do not have much opportunity for women in management positions; others do. Your participation in such things depends on your own particular denomination and your personal convictions.

Then there are the more "domestic" kinds of jobs. Don't look down on these as "women's work," as they are very important. There is the "Dorcas ministry." Dorcas used her sewing talent to clothe the poor widows and their children and other needy people in the seaport city of Joppa. She died suddenly one day in the midst of her ministry. Peter came several days later and raised her from the dead (Acts 9:36-41). Obviously, God wanted her ministry to continue. Women through the years have been inspired to help others in this same way after reading about a disciple named Dorcas.

Another "ministry of helps" is in serving the altar of the church. In some churches, these women are called the Altar Guild. Their ministry is similar to that of certain priests of the Old Testament who were chosen to care for the tabernacle or tent which was, in those days, the focal place of worship.

Perhaps you are an amateur florist, and can

---

*See Jay Adams, *Competent to Counsel*, cited earlier on p. 80.

serve the Lord by making the altar beautiful through your talent. Many bouquets from the altar have gone to cheer the sick.

You may have a ministry of hospitality, making your home available to missionaries and visiting speakers. A Seattle couple built two or three extra bedrooms onto their home to be used for this purpose. The Book of Hebrews reminds us, "Be not forgetful to entertain strangers: for thereby some have entertained angels unawares" (13:2). A widow is reported for her good works, "if she has lodged strangers, if she has washed the saints' feet" (I Tim. 5:10).

Now let's look at some of the things a woman can do on a wider scope than serving in the local church.

You may discover you have hidden talent in the field of writing. Try writing your testimony for a magazine.* When witnessing to someone you may not see again, knowing you have not quite said all you wanted to, it's good to be able to give them a copy of a magazine with your testimony in it. Many Christians are writing today, flooding the market with good literature, helping to counteract the flood of sick and destructive writing.

Do you love languages? The Wycliffe Bible Translators may have a job for you. Even though the New Testament has been translated into 1,000 languages, it is estimated there are still some 2,000 lan-

*Aglow Magazine is interested in articles and testimonies by women. For further information, write to Katie Fortune, editor, 7715 - 236th S. W., Edmonds, Wash., 98020.

guages to go** to spread the Gospel throughout the world before the return of Jesus Christ. Jesus said, "And this gospel of the kingdom shall be preached in *all* the world for a witness unto all nations; and then shall the end come" (Matt. 24:14).

Christian artists are needed to help turn the current trend from the weird to the divine. If you are not an artist, perhaps you can do creative crafts. Connie, a friend of mine whose father was an artist, never felt she had the talent he had and was discouraged from even trying. After she received the power of the Holy Spirit, she began to use the little artistic ability she had ignored. Connie's house now is creatively decorated with cardboard collage plaques, decoupage pictures from old masters prints or even especially meaningful birthday or Christmas cards, dried flower arrangements and so forth. At present, she teaches a Bible class in conjunction with crafts for the "Creative Woman." Women who never believed they had any artistic ability are amazed at what they can learn to do with God's help.* Dawn, another friend, makes interesting clay-baked crosses which are very original and can be found in many Seattle boutiques. And Jane paints words like "love" and "joy" on driftwood or smooth stones she brings home from the beach of Puget Sound.

**Ethel E. Wallis and Mary A. Bennett, *Two Thousand Tongues to Go* (New York, N.Y.: Harper and Row, 1959).

*A book that elaborates on women's hidden talents is *Hidden Art* by Edith Schaeffer (Wheaton, Illinois: Tyndale House, 1971).

If you have even a small amount of musical talent, God can put it to good use. An increasing number of people with little or no musical training have found the Holy Spirit giving them new songs and choruses, inspiring many thousands of people. As my husband and I travel, we are constantly learning many such new songs. I particularly enjoy singing Scripture set to music.

Perhaps you have a pleasing voice and personality. You might start a radio or television program. Taking a course in communications at a local university or college would help you determine if you're talented in these fields. The growing number of Christian TV stations will be looking for some good programming.*

How's that for some "do's" instead of don'ts"? These are just a few ideas. There are certainly many more, including some very important ones I haven't mentioned. I'm sure now that you'll think of others.

---

*The miracle story of CBN is told in Pat Robertson's *Shout It from the Housetops* (Plainfield, N. J.: Logos International, 1972).

EPILOGUE

Dear Reader,

Now is my chance to write you a letter. I've enjoyed trying to answer these questions, perhaps they were yours also. If you are in a situation similar to some of the ones discussed in these pages, yet the answer given doesn't seem the right one for you, don't worry. There is no "pat" answer for every similar situation. Each life is intricately complex and different.

John 16:13-14 proclaims that the Holy Spirit will lead you into *all* truth. Count on this as you wait upon the Lord and seek to know His will. Whatever your unique problem is, the Lord Jesus has the solution for it, and the Holy Spirit is here to reveal Jesus' words to you.

May God bless you. *Maranatha!*

For a free copy of
LOGOS JOURNAL
send your name and address to
Logos Journal
Box 191
Plainfield, New Jersey 07060
and say, "one free Journal, please."